GOING
ALIC

GW01045200

NativeSpain™.com

GOING NATIVE IN ALICANTE

Susan Bearder

NativeSpain.™com

To Fay who gave me my first home in Alicante and just loved exploring with me.

Acknowledgements

I'd just like to say a big thank you to all the people who generously shared their time and stories. They are: Steve Halls *(www.thisispain.com)*, Rod Ross *(www.homeinvest-intl.es)*, Vernon Grant, Favel (Fay) Hill, Margaret from Geneva, Gaile Griffin Peers *(www.javeaphotos.com)*, Sharon Richards *(www.livespainforlife.com)*, Colin Wiffen *(www.costablancaholiday.info)*, Garry Holland *(www.eels-sp.com)*, Alberto Kramer and Jackie Orford.

Also, thanks go to Gaile Griffin Peers and Gary A Wright (at *www.javeaphotos.com*) for their permission to use their brilliant photograph for the cover as well as Alberto Kramer, who provided the beautiful photograph for the back cover and a couple of additional photographs that you'll find later in this book.

Contents

RESOURCES

ABOUT SUSAN BEARDER

INDEX

Overview

INTRODUCTION

Say "Alicante" to anyone and will your version of what constitutes "Alicante" tie up with theirs? Probably not. It certainly doesn't rate very highly in the main guide books to Spain. A major oversight, in our opinion, which we hope to rectify with this book.

This fascinating area of Eastern Spain on the Mediterranean is known as the Costa Blanca. However it is much more than the Costa Blanca, although that's where the population is at its densest. Alicante or Alicant in Valencian (a dialect of Catalan) is the capital of the province but San Juan de Alicante is the largest in terms of population density.

It's been really fascinating researching this guide. When I started this task for NativeSpain I realised there is a whole major area not really covered by other guides particularly Monovar, Elda, Novelda, Sax and La Romana. As I house hunted this area with deadly seriousness I know it very well.

Whilst backtracking and researching I found out such a lot of new stuff that I have my own NativeSpain "To Do" list planned out. I'm happy to say it will take me years to complete, this area is so interesting... I know that if you don't travel into the hills and mountains, wander the pueblos and towns, or visit beyond Alicante or Benidorm you will never truly experience the real Spain of passion and an enviable *alegría de la vida*.

ALICANTE AT A GLANCE

To try to explain the structure of Alicante we have to start with the Community of Valencia. This name in itself is pretty confusing but basically the Community consists of three provinces of which Alicante is the most southern (the other two being Valencia and Castellón).

Alicante Province

The province has a population of over 451,000 according to the 2006 census. The coastline famed as the Costa Blanca is 200kms long. There are basically three major areas within the province but there is also a loose structure of nine subdivisions known as comarcas:

Comtat: Cocentaina is the main town.

Alcoià: has two different sub areas Valls d'Alcoi, of which Alcoy is its main town and Hoya de Castalla.

Marina Alta: Dénia is the principle town and apparently the rainiest.

Marina Baixa or **Marina Baja:** Benidorm being the principle town.

Alto Vinalopó or **Alt Vinalopó:** Villena and Sax being two of the main towns.

Vinalopó Mitjà or **Vinalopó Medio:** Elda is the principle town.

Baix Vinalopó or **Bajo Vinalopó:** which includes Elche, Crevillent and Santa Pola.

L'Alacantí: Principle towns are Alicante and San Juan de Alicante.

Vega Baja del Segura or **Baix Segura:** Orihuela and Torrevieja are two of the principle towns.

Okay! So now we might be talking about the same place. If you have already gone native, would like to go native in this area of Spain or just want to be able to go native for a long weekend - *"hacer un puente"* - I hope there is something for everyone in this guide to the Alicante Province.

One of the most important things to remember if you want to go native in Alicante is that you have to get stuck in and do some of the things that the Spanish do.

A BRIEF HISTORY

The Shaping of Alicante

Any website or guidebook you happen to come upon is likely to give you at least a part view of the history and development of Alicante as a city and Alicante as a province. It is the work of the academics to find the actual sources of the material that is written about this area but I guess I should do my version of why this province is as it is, so bearing in mind I am an enthusiastic amateur here is my potted take.

The Iberians are the oldest documented peoples in this area - unfortunately they have not been well covered in the prehistory of the world. Slowly this changing and the Iberians are being given their due importance with websites such as *www.celtiberia.net* documenting their history.

Some of my best sources of information come from my daughter who specialised in archaeology and anthropology.

Prehistory

The Prehistory of the Iberian peninsula begins with the arrival of the first hominins (the tribe of the great apes) around a million years ago and ends with the Punic Wars, when the territory enters the domains of written history.

In this long period some of its most significant landmarks were to host the last stand of the Neanderthal people, to develop impressive Paleolithic art, and with southern France, to become the seat of the earliest civilizations of Western Europe.

C.4700 BC

Cardium Pottery Neolithic culture (imprinting of the clay with a shell motif), also known as Mediterranean Neolithic, arrives in Eastern Iberia. While some remains of this culture have been found as far west as Portugal, its distribution is basically Mediterranean (Catalonia, Valencian region, Ebro valley, Balearic islands).

The first settlements in the area were centred around the slopes of mount Benacantil, occupied today by the castle of Santa Bárbara.

C. 1000 BC

By 1000BC the Greeks and Phoenicians found the area around Guardamar perfect for their needs of seafaring and trading.

C. 600 BC

By the sixth century BC, the rival armies of Carthage and Rome began to invade and fight for control of the Iberian Peninsula. The Carthaginian general Hamilcar established the fortified settlement of Akra Leuke, where Alicante stands today.

AD 713

Probably the most powerful influence felt in the province is the legacy of the Moors. The Islamic influence extended to Alicante and the region was to become part of Al-Andalus.

The Moors brought with them science and the arts, mathematics and astronomy, music, poetry, foods which are now staple to this region at a time when the rest of Europe was in the Dark Ages.

The Day The Universe Changed

"...at first, the land resembled the rest of Europe in all its squalor. But within two-hundred years the Moors had turned Al-Andalus into a bastion of culture, commerce and beauty.

"Irrigation systems imported from Syria and Arabia turned the dry plains... into an agricultural cornucopia. Olives and wheat had always grown there. The Arabs added pomegranates, oranges, lemons, aubergines, artichokes, cumin, coriander, bananas, almonds, pams, henna, woad, madder, saffron, sugar-cane, cotton, figs, grapes, peaches, apricots and rice."

The Day the Universe Changed, James Burke, 1985, p. 37

AD 1244

The Christian Kings began to systematically reconquer the different parts. The names of the kings Ferdinand, Jaime, and Alfonso come to the fore. Alicante is split between Castile and Aragon in 1244 under the Treaty of Almizra.

Alicante's name, Arabic for 'The City of Light', is one of the remnants from this period. The Muslim reign lasted until the 13th century when King Jaime I recaptured the city and made it part of his newly created Kingdom of Valencia.

So it puts into focus why these major re-enactments all over the province these days, of the battles between the Moors and Christians, are a mirror of the past on the present.

More Dates

In 1490 Ferdinand II creates the city of Alicante.

1609 to 1614 King Felipe III expels many Moriscos, losing thousands of skilled artisans and agricultural labourers.

In 1691 the French bombard the city for seven days.

During the War of the Spanish Succession (1701-1714) the British destroy the Castilo of Santa Barbara.

1858 saw the arrival of the railway, linking Alicante to central Spain.

Correspondence with Bernard Cornwell and his Official site

Dear Bernard: I am currently editing/writing for "Going Native in Alicante" and have put the Sharpe novels in the suggested reading list. I am currently reading Sharpe's Fury and found myself nosing through your books in Spanish at the National Library in Madrid as they are promoting them as background to the 200 Year Anniversary of the Peninsular Wars. (There is a fabulous expo in said library by the way; Goya prints and an amazing cartoon of a British soldier with woman and child and washing drying on his rifle as they march.)

Is there any particular episode of Sharpe that related to Valencia or Alicante in particular as I know there was an attack on the castillo in Alicante by the British? Much obliged and keep writing. Susan Bearder

A: I can't think of any episode! But perhaps I should write one? And thank you for reminding me of that Goya print! OK! Sharpe must march to Valencia and Alicante! Gracias!

So I for one am watching that Sharpe space - I don't know about you...

Modern History

By the early 20th century the whole of Spain was almost at the point of revolution. Amid growing political unrest, King Alfonso XIII abdicated the throne, and in 1931 a Spanish Republic was declared.

In 1936, General Francisco Franco led an uprising, supported by Fascist Italy and Nazi Germany, to re-establish the authority of the Catholic church, the army and the aristocracy. After three years of bloody civil war, Franco's armies were victorious. Alicante was one of the last cities loyal to the government to be overcome.

Alicante was the target of some vicious air bombings during the three years of civil conflict, most remarkably the bombing by the Italian Aviazione Legionaria of the Mercado de Abastos in May 25, 1938 in which more than 300 civilians died.

The next 20 years under Franco's police state were incredibly difficult, with severe frosts in 1941 and 1946 adding to the problems of local orange farmers.

The late 1950s and early 1960s saw the onset of a lasting transformation of the region due to tourism. Large buildings and complexes rose in Albufereta and Playa de San Juan, with the climate being the best tool to bring prospective buyers and tourists who kept hotels reasonably busy. The tourist development also brought other industry such as restaurants, bars and businesses focused on visitors.

Franco died in 1975 and his successor King Juan Carlos I guiding Spain towards a democratic constitutional monarchy.

Alicante port has been reinventing itself since the industrial decline the city suffered in the 1980s. In recent years, the Port Authority has established it as one of the most important ports in Spain for cruises, with 72 calls to port made by cruises in 2007 bringing some 80,000 cruise passengers and 30,000 crew to the city each year.

FAMOUS PEOPLE FROM ALICANTE

A great site for Alicante's famous people is: *www.alicantevivo.org*

George Washington Montgomery (1804-1841) born in Alicante, was United States diplomat and editor/publisher of the first Spanish language translation of the works of Washington Irving.

The group **Los Alcarson** – let them speak or sing for themselves! Listen to a Podcast from 40 years ago courtesy of Alicante Vivo at: *www.alicantevivo.podomatic.com/entry/2008-02-02T01_30_52-08_00*

Carlos Arniches (1866 - died in Madrid 1943) Dramatist best known for the one-act zarzuela (musical comedy) and one-act sainete (sketches). He wrote 270 of these and was a master of observation based on the language and customs of the lower classes of Madrid where they still celebrate this art form (theatre de Zarzuela).

Rafael Altamira y Crevea (1866-1951) co-founder of Permanent Court of International Justice so-called the "World Court", after 1945 called the International Court of Justice.

Francisco Javier de Balmis (1753-1819) physician who headed the Balmis expedition to vaccinate the Spanish-colonies (in the Canary Islands, Colombia, Ecuador, Peru, Mexico, the Philippines and China) population against smallpox.

Antonio Gades_(1936-2004) Flamenco dancer and film star. Born in Elda but moved to Madrid. Given the name of Gades by Pilar Lopez. He travelled the world and performed in many of Federico Garcia Lorca's works. He married a number of times (Fidel Castro was best man at one of his weddings which tells you about Gades' politics). In 1963 he performed with Carmen Amaya (extremely famous female flamenco dancer) in a film called Los Tarantos.

Juan Gil-Albert (1904-1994) Writer and poet born in Alcoy. Anti-fascist, he went into self exile 1936-1947. Later on his return he continues his work and stays totally separated from the fascist regime but in time receives the Medalla al Merito de Bellas Artes, given an honorary doctorate by the University of Alicante and became a favoured son of Alcoy.

Figueras Pachego (1880-1960) Alicante, was a man of letters and wrote much on the city of Alicante.

Belen Rueda film actress and TV presenter; lived for a while as a child in Alicante although born in Madrid. Winner of a Goya for "The Orphanage" 2007.

Miguel Hernandez (1910-1942) Poet, poor goatherd and farmhand from Orihuela, Alicante. It is considered that he wrote his best poetry while imprisoned during the Civil War. One of his poems, 'Llegó con tres heridas' (He came with three wounds), is a popular song, recorded by Joan Baez on her 'Gracias a La Vida' album.

Translations of the first lines of two of his famous poems:

"I live in shadow filled with light…"

"The bull knows at the end…"

On the wall next to his bed in prison whilst dying of tuberculosis, he wrote his final lines *"Goodbye, brothers, comrades, friends: let me take my leave of the sun and the fields"*.

Other famous Alicante natives include: **Gabriel Miró** (1879-1930) novelist; **Juan Escarré** (1969) field hockey player; **Miriam Blasco** Olympic Judo champion; **Isabel Fernandez** Olympic Judo champion; **Vanessa Romero** model and actress; **Maria Jurado** model and actress; **Esther Cañadas** model and actress; **Pedro Ferrándiz** basketball coach; **Hannibal Laguna** fashion designer; **Francisco Rufete** footballer. Born in Benejuzar, midfielder for Valencia and won three Spanish caps.

LANGUAGE

Alicante province, as part of the autonomous kingdom of Valencia has two official languages; Spanish and Valencian, which explains some of the confusions of spelling. This is, however, a real example of the region's heritage and history and worth knowing a little about.

A regional survey in 2005 showed that less than 40% of Castellón, Valencia and Alicante now use Valencian at home and even less with their friends. With the sharp increase of incomers there are now many residents who say they have no understanding of Valencian. There are sub-dialects within the region aswell. The past and future of the Valencian language is complex and still of political importance.

Valencian - Language or Catalan Dialect?

Valencian (valencià) is the historical, traditional, and official name used in the Valencian Community of Spain to refer to the region's native language, known elsewhere as Catalan.

There is consensus amongst linguists that Valencian is the common name for the Catalan language as spoken in the Valencian Community.

Specifically, Valencian is the most distinctive and established Western variety, with a written tradition which started as early as the 15th century. It can be then distinguished from the other major standard, the "Catalan of Barcelona" or Central Catalan group of varieties.

However some in Valencia, refusing the academic consensus, use Valencian (especially *llengua valenciana*, "Valencian language") to refer to this variety as if it were different from the Catalan language as a whole. These theories are usually supported by politicians rather than linguists. They are mostly based on disputing the origin of the language in Valencia.

Other Sources of Information

Acadèmia Valenciana de la Llengua
www.avl.gva.es

Ethnologue: Languages of the World
www.ethnologue.com

Spanish Language School in Alicante
www.zadorspain.com

CULTURE
MUSEUMS

MARQ – The Archaeological Museum in Alicante let's you get a taste for archaeological remains dating from the pre-history Palaeolithic age right up to the modern age. Entry is just €3. *www.marqalicante.com*, Plaza Doctor Gómez Ulla, Alicante T: 965 149 000

MUBAG – The Gravina Mueseum of Art, opened in 2001, shows art from the Alicante area from the 16th century. Free entry. *www.mubag.org* 13-15 Calle Gravina, Alicante T: 965 146 780

MACA – Museum of Contemporary Art, La Casa de la Asegurada includes work from Juan Miró, Salvador Dalí, Pablo Picasso, Juan Gris and Julio González. Closed for works until, the Summer of 2009. Free entry. Plaza de Santa Maria, 3, Alicante T: 965 140 959.

Valencian Folk dancers

EVENTS AND CELEBRATIONS

Fiestas and Festivals are ongoing all year round. Here is a summary of some of the more important ones but see each town's own entry for small, localised events including the Moors and Christians.

Las Fallas - Fire Festival

This festival marks the start of Spring in the Valencian area and usually falls between the 16th and 19th of

13

March. The "fallas" are papier-mâché models depicting satirical scenes which are then set fire to on the Nit de Foc (the night of the fire). Benidorm stages its own version of the famous event.

Semana Santa

Easter celebrations are incredibly important in Spain. They will actually last for more than a week, Good Friday to Easter Sunday. Torrevieja parades are very good. The town traffic will become strangled while the parade is in progress, so be warned.

Los Fogueres

Another fire festival, features in a number of towns in the region and marks the Summer Solstice from the 20th June. It is classed as one of the official celebrations of Alicante and consists of elaborate floats (that get burnt), bonfires, firecrackers, barracas (many temporary bars), concerts and a beauty contest (the Fire Beauties), where all the contestants wear traditional embroidered costumes. *www.hogueras.org*

Los Santos Innocentes

28th December is the equivalent of April Fools Day in UK.

Feast of the Three Kings

You may need to adjust your ideas about Christmas if you are going to go "native" as in Spain there really are Twelve Days of Christmas.

December 24th – for families this evening meal is usually spent at home.

December 25th – a quiet religious day.

December 31st - January 1 - very noisy celebration of the New Year. They eat one grape on each stroke of the clock to see the New Year in. There's also a little matter of red knickers... Supposed to bring good luck to the wearer.

January 5th - Feast of the Three Kings celebrating the bearing of gifts to the Christ child is reflected by gifts to each other.

Finally, I couldn't resist mentioning the Valencian festival of La Tomatina in Buñol. On the last Wednesday in August there's a massive tomato fight with a cast of thousands, would you believe.

Other Cultural Events

There is so much going on you have to do your research in advance to get the most out of a stay, use the following websites to help you.

Sign up for news from *www.ticktackticket.com* to get advance warning of concerts coming up in Spain and a means of buying tickets early.

Alicante tourist site is updated regularly *www.alicanteturismo.com*

The tourist office for the whole region of Valencia has great content too (*www.comunitatvalenciana.com*) including an excellent downloadable newsletter in English.

Finally, new stuff is being added all the time at *www.nativespain.com*

ACTIVITIES

In this section we want to give you an idea of the range of activities available to you in the Alicante Province. Before you come out check on this site - *www.atrapalo.com* - for some bargains.

"Jefe" - A well respected elder of Villajoyosa   © Alberto Kramer

To Do

<u>Ballooning</u> – For someone who normally gets vertigo I love this form of transport, this is the perfect getaway for three hours. *www.aeroglobo.com*

<u>Bullfighting</u> – Bah! All over the place during summer.

<u>Dancing</u> – Do a Spanish dance class; learn salsa, merengue, bachata, reguetón at Playa San Juan. *www.webnaturola.com* If dancing isn't for you go and watch someone else do it.

<u>Diving</u> – Diving on the Costa Blanca is fun and relatively inexpensive. Most dive clubs cater for beginners ("trydive") through to all levels of qualification. You could try *www.deniamar.com* in Dénia, *www.diveacademy-santapola.com* in Santa Pola or *www.divingmediterraneo.com* in Torrevieja, *www.javeadivers.com* in Jávea to mention just a few.

<u>Equine matters</u> – Horses and horse breeding are a very big part of Spanish life. For trekking, lessons or to ride around in a horse and cart, try *www.ondараridingschool.com* near Javea.

<u>Freebies</u> - Check for free events especially during the summer. For jazz around Alicante for instance there is Desden Jazz y Mas on the Centro Commerical in the University area at San Vicente del Raspais. See *www.desden.es* for more details.

<u>Rent a Bike</u> – This is usually very economical. You could try *www.i-lovebike.com* - they have all sorts available (motor-powered and pedal-powered!)

<u>Summer Programmes</u> - Many towns run concerts and dance events in the town centres during the summer months so call into your local tourist office once in a while to keep up with what's going on.

<u>Tennis</u> - With Rafael Nadal the new golden boy of tennis it's worth thinking about the academies and coaching available around Alicante Province. Many of the hotels have courts and if your kids are a little more serious about the game, enrol them on a tennis holiday with the Spanish Language school *www.zadorspain.com* - they'll come back with a great serve and a local accent!

Treats - What about a spa visit? Search on www.dormirenbalnearios.com for a full list of spas, there are 13 to choose from. The only natural thermal Spa is at Aigües which is about to get an enormous face lift or you could take a day out and slip over the border to Archena Spa in Murcia for the total health experience.

Walking - Part of a major Spanish walking route (GR 7) passes through the province taking in Pinoso to Fredes. Sierra de Carche near Pinoso and north west of Sax, is a very natural area with lovely walking. Nearly got to live here - nice house in wrong place.

Climbing & Canyoning – For climbing and abseiling in the numerous barrancos in the Las Marinas alta and baja visit *www.costablancamountainfriends.com*. Canyoning is the descent of natural gorges by a mixture of hiking, scrambling, swimming and abseiling. Or *www.aqua-ventura.com* who offer everything for families and more adventurous groups, from climbing, kayaking, canyoning, yachting, paragliding, mountain-biking and probably other things as well! There's also Adrian Bates' site: *www.geocities.com/costablancaclimbing* for all climbing related activities.

Football - Alicante Province have two second division clubs, Hercules and Elche both local to the area of Alicante and deadly rivals. Each looking for a good position at the top of the league as the season ends. Local football is followed passionately and if you are a "hincha" (football fan) you might like to find out what is going on wherever you are – you may be very pleasantly surprised at the standard.

To Watch

<u>Cycling</u> - Valencia Cycling Tour during February and March. Five stages through the Valencian Community. This is a very important sport in Spain. Town centres are closed for the event.

<u>Motor Cycling</u> - Grand Prix Valencia in November. Big, big event brings many people into the area from all over Europe. 2007's final race was won by Pedrosa of Spain on a Honda.

<u>Motor Racing F1</u> - One of the world's premier events The Valencia Street Circuit Grand Prix held in August is quickly sold out.

<u>Yachting</u> - Volvo "Round the World" Race is happening 2008-2009. The biggest offshore race there is! In October 2008 Alicante was the starting point. *www.volvooceanrace.org*. The 33rd America's Cup may be held in Valencia.

For The Kids

<u>Safari Aitana near Penaguila</u> – This is a substantial drive from the coast and quite slow-going. The ticket gets you into a drive-through safari-type park and a second enclosure for walking through. I noted big hee-haw noises as I went to the restaurant bar. (Quite reasonable) Current ticket costs €17 for adult and €12 for children. Hours open 11:00-19:00.

If you don't like animals in captivity then just enjoy the drive up the mountain from El Campello or Villajoyosa and down the other side to Alcoy. Have a picnic up at the top under the trees. *www.safariaitana.com*

<u>Terra Mitica</u> – This is a major theme park in Benidorm, which consists of five distinct themes; Egypt - Land of Pharaohs; Greece - The Home of the Gods; Rome - The Frontier; Iberia - The Warm Shores and The Islands - The

Great Journey. Terra Mitica seems to provide excellent value for money with a Season Pass, allowing unlimited visits and use of rides throughout the season. Group booking discounts are available all year round. The 2008 ticket price guide is very complicated and I am not even going to try to explain it. But here is the website so you can see for yourself. Tickets can be purchased online. Terra Mitica juniors are children between the ages of 5 and 10, seniors are people 60 years and over and children under the age of 4 enter the park for free all year round. Visit *www.terramiticapark.com*

Terra Natura - Lies in a vast area of mountainside next to its better known neighbour, Terra Mitica. Although the theme park has over 700 metres of water slides it is essentially an animal park divided according to continent. Each continent sector is home to the animals, people and vegetation native to it. You'll even find typical dishes of the region in that sector's restaurants.

Within each sector there are a selection of interesting shows and rides. You can take a train ride around the park or for the more adventurous take a Tarzan like trip over the elephant enclosure on a zip wire. And if you survive how about going swimming with baby sharks!

Entrance to Terra Natura is charged separately from the water park though you'll see offers in Benidorm which include the water park in a "two parks for the price of one" offer. Look out for people giving out flyers on the promenade of Playa Levante which give each person €5 to spend in the Terra Natura shop. Check the Terra Natura website for the latest entrance fees, opening times and special offers. Visit *www.terranatura.com*

Mundomar – A marine and exotic park with a dolphinarium in Benidorm. It is twinned with Aqualandia next door. The main Show of the day is a 40-minute spectacular water ballet with a team of synchronised swimmers among the dolphins. There are also flamingos, turtles, parrots and penguins. Visit *www.mundomar.es*

Day Trips

Tabarca Island - Go to Tabarca Island by ferry from Alicante or Santa Pola, take your swimming and snorkelling gear and enjoy a menu del día. 9 sailings per day in the summer, and just €13 for adults and €11 for children for the 30 minute crossing. *www.turismosantapola.es*

Ibiza by boat - Go to Ibiza by boat from Alicante or Dénia. Trasmediterranea's link takes less than three hours – if you are clever you could have a mini cruise by picking the boat up on its return leg from Palma to Ibiza to Alicante. *www.trasmediterranea.es*

Montgó Natural Park - An imposing limestone mountain rises up 750m from the plain just a few hundred metres from the sea and almost parallel to the coastline between Dénia and neighbouring Jávea. Montgó is home to over 600 different species of plants such as the red lavender and Valencia rock violet, some of which are unique to this area. You can climb to the top of Montgó from all sides which is an enjoyable journey through a varied landscape of crops, pine forests, scrub land and rocky areas with caves. There are special walks graded low to medium difficulty and all are marked out. Take a picnic and enjoy the breathtaking panoramic views of the surrounding area. The island of Ibiza can be seen on a clear day. *www.parquesnaturales.gva.es*

Cuevas De Canelobre - the caves lie on the northern side of the mountain Cabeçó d' Or (near Busot) and resemble the nave of a cathedral. Over the course of time the rocks assumed bizarre shapes and the acoustics within the grotto are fantastic. When you've had enough of the darkness enjoy a walking-tour in the vicinity. Afterwards food is available in one of Busot's restaurants. The cave can be reached via the A7 or the N332 (exit El Campello) and then towards Busot.

Camping

There are plenty of campsites in the area, including:

Medieval Campsite - In Alfaz del Pi, a medieval environment with first class facilities: electricity, water and drainage in every plot. You can enjoy medieval performances such as jousting! Visit *www.camping-medieval.com* or call them T: 966 867 139

There are more than 10 campsites in the **Benidorm** area, including:

www.camping-arenablanca.es, T: 965 861 889
www.campingvillamar.com, T: 966 811 255
www.campingbenidorm.net, T: 965 860 011

In **El Campello** there's:

www.campingcostablanca.com, T: 965 630 670
www.campings.com/camping-pinosalicante-denia
www.campingsonline.com/elmolino
www.camping-villasol.com

www.campingmarjal.com – the website tells you about facilities for disabled people and costs for pet owners.

www.campinglamarina.com – 5 star rating and full services for variety of requirements including disabled people and visitors with pets.

Finally, there's **Los Llanos** near **Dénia**, with wooden cabins, apartments and pitches. *www.losllanos.net* T: 965 755 188

Evenings/Nights

The Costa Blanca is a great place for nightlife. Most of the towns will have bars, restaurants and clubs open till the small hours, especially during the summer months.

Starting with Benidorm, there's the Benidorm Palace *www.benidorm-palace.com*. If you like cabaret or comedy then this is the nightspot to visit. For other cabaret shows try out The Rich Bitch Bar, Valentines or the Talk of the Coast.

If you've watched the popular television programme, *Benidorm*, then you'll have been subjected to the phenomenon "Sticky Vicky", a sixty odd year old woman who, nakedly performs a series of 'magic' acts and tricks with ping-pong balls, razor blades and beer bottles, using parts of the body not usually seen in regular magic shows! Look for local adverts to see where she's performing.

The casino is just outside Benidorm on the way to Villajoyosa (approx 10km). There are 38 slot machines and 23 games tables with roulette, American roulette, black jack, chemin de fer, punto y blanco etc. As with all casinos in Benidorm you must have Photo ID such as a driving licence or Passport to enter. The casino is open till the small hours every night and there is a small entrance fee.

A great website for all Benidorm nightlife is: *www.benidorm-spotlight.com*

If you are up for a bit of partying, Alicante is a great place. The main drinking area is called "El barrio", which is the old quarter of the city and consists of hundreds of bars with an excellent variety of music and atmosphere. Bars normally stay open until 4am. El Barrio is just behind the *Rambla* and down from the *Plaza San Cristobal*. Try Havana Caf, Desafinado or for techno and house music there's Z Klub.

The smart new Alicante marina has no shortage of drinking spots either: *www.alicante-spotlight.com*

FOOD AND DRINK

The following section has been contributed by Steve my partner. You know that saying: "the way to a man's heart is through his stomach"? Well this is his explanation of why he has fallen in love with Spain and the Southern Mediterranean in particular.

Eating Like a Native

Meal times are very important to the Spanish. The whole event is not just for sustenance but it is also a social/family occasion. Usually 3, 4 or 5 leisurely courses spent over 2 or 3 hours with much talking and laughter.

The main meal of the day is lunch starting at approximately 14:00. Spanish restaurants and most bars prepare a menu of the day (menu del día) which is usually 3 or 4 courses with a choice of fare and very reasonably priced. A typical menu will be salad and/or soup, main course (fish or meat or vegetarian) and dessert, served with a basket of fresh bread and washed down with water, wine or beer and coffee and all for 8 – 12Euros. It may cost a bit more if you go really upmarket.

If you prefer to eat your main meal in the evening then remember the Spanish, having had a good meal at lunch time, eat much later than the average northern European, often not starting to appear until 22:00 especially during the summertime. Remember most will not have finished work until 20:00. And don't be surprised to see very young children or even babies out with mum and dad and maybe even grandma and pa at this time of night.

Tapas

Tapas, the word meaning "lid", are a traditional snack or light meal. There are often numerous choices including vegetarian options on display on the bar or counter. However a small tapa, *"a pincho"* is often free when served alongside a drink.

This is how Coronita beer developed the tradition of having a slice of lemon in the top of the bottle - stops flies and dust getting in.

Tapas are normally served on saucer-sized plates so you may decide you need 2 or 3 different ones to get your fill. They are almost always served with a basket of fresh bread. This is a more expensive way to eat but fun and allows you to try different and local things. If you like fish always try these options but be warned the Spanish like garlic a lot!

A good meat option is *albondigas* (meatballs) and the *tortillas* are particularly good (a Spanish *tortilla* is normally like a thick omelette with potatoes and onion.) Ask for *un ración* (a racion) if you prefer a larger amount of your favourite.

Drinking Like a Native

You will be hard pushed to find a drunken Spaniard as you'll notice the natives take their time, always eat when they drink and consume far more *agua* (water) than us Brits. Also the legal drink driving alcohol limit is lower than most countries, certainly the UK's. So go native and enjoy yourself sensibly.

Coffee is also very important to the Spanish and is served all day and night. Once you have experienced coffee in Spain you will become aware of how poor most UK coffee is. Try a *belmonte* – coffee, brandy (Spanish which is much weaker than French) and condensed milk – naughty but nice!

Cerveza (beer or normally lager) is always served very cold and generally in smallish glasses. Some bars serve the *cerveza* in glasses taken directly from a freezer to make your beer extra cold. Delicious on a hot day.

I am an addict for my morning *café con leche* and I also love Ines Rosales anise biscuits which can be bought all over the place, although they originate from Seville. If you have cholesterol problems enjoy a little *churros* but if not hey pig out with chocolate as well.

Many people agree that beer/lager is better from the tap and it is no different in Spain. Ask for a caña (small glass) or vaso for a larger glass.

Food and drink are worthy of celebration here in Spain and Alicante province takes its place with the best.

Wine

Wines come in two styles, normal and DOC, which implies that the wine only comes from a particular area, with a particular set of grapes and that the conditions of production are controlled.

The DOC (Denominación de Origen) wine region of Alicante covers 51 towns in the province of Alicante from two different areas: Alicante and La Marina.

Alicante wines are very fruity with a wide variety of grapes, which are used to make reds and whites (dry and sweet). Red wine grape varieties: Bobal, Cabernet Sauvignon, Merlot, Tempranillo, Pinot Noir and of course Monastrell. White wine grape varieties: Chardonnay, Moscatel Romano, Planta Fina and Merseguera.

Two of the area's most representative wines are *Fondillón* and *Tinto*.

El Fondillón: a mellow wine, with high alcohol content, made with the Monastrell grape, ideal served as a dessert wine. It has been named by the EEC (together with Port, Sherry and Champagne) as a high quality wine. You can buy this wine in any of the co-operative wine producers in Monóvar. This was a favourite with the Spanish Monarchs from the 16th Century.

Tinto: wine produced on a small scale and often compared to French wines; the young ones have an intense ruby colour which changes to amber as they get older. With a fruity nose, they are known for their freshness and strength, try some made in the village of Parcent (Bodegas Gutierrez de la Vega).

If you want to try a dessert wine or take back a present of a bottle of dessert wine, I recommend you go for a sweet Moscatel from Marina Alta, pop to the town of Teulada to buy some.

Lovely Local Produce

Mediterranean vegetables should be eaten when in season.

English	Spanish	Season
Artichokes	alcachofa	November - April
Asparagus	espárrago	March - April
Broad Beans	habas	Mid-March - May
Courgettes	calabacines	May - July
Fennel	hinojo	November - January
Grapes	uvas	September -November
New potatoes	potatas	June - August
Melons	melones	June - August
Peas	guisantes	March - April
Peppers	pimientas	July - August
Quince	membrillo	September - November
Sweetcorn	maíz dulce	June - July
Tomatoes	tomates	April - July
Pomegranates	granadas	October - March
Lemons	limones	December – February
Oranges	naranjas	December – February

Broad beans are eaten raw, without ceremony, in Spanish bars. When they're in season there will be a pile on the bar. Just throw the shells on the floor to join the ever-growing mountain!

Alicante Food Specialities

While Paella is the best-known Spanish rice dish, the province of Alicante has many dishes of its own. Many of the restaurants are called *arrocerias* or rice restaurants. Some of the more popular dishes are as follows; *Arroz a la banda* (made with fish and stewed in fish stock, see recipe later), *Arroz a la Alicantina* (chicken and rice with shellfish and dried red pepper), *Caldero* (stewed rice with fish, wetter dish), *El Arroz con Costra* (rice with baked egg on top), *Arroz Negro* (with squid in its own ink), and *Arroz con Conejo* (rice with rabbit).

Make time to pick an orange directly from a tree, smell it, eat it, love it.

Seafood is also popular due to many fishermen operating out of Alicante and other seaside towns dotted along the coastline. Typical fish caught here are Sardines, Red Mullet, Tuna, Anchovies and *Palayas* (small plaice). Shellfish includes red prawns (can be very expensive!), cuttlefish, octopus and squid.

I particularly enjoy *Arroz a la banda*. The reason this is so good is due to the preparation of the rice and broth. My cookbook on the food and wines of Spain (Penelope Casas: "*The Foods and Wines of Spain*") quotes a recipe from a beachside cafe called *El Pegoli* from 25 year ago. I hope the restaurant is still there!

Arroz a Banda

Cook about 300g of shrimps in their shells in salted water for about two minutes. Drain and shell the shrimps.

Make a fish broth with a pound of cleaned whiting or similar, a bay leaf, half a cup of white wine, sprigs of parsley, sliced onion, lemon slice, salt and 6 black peppercorns, and any left overs from shrimp shell preparation and reserve the cooking liquid, a cup of clam juice. Add enough water for six servings. Bring to the boil, cover and simmer for at least 90 minutes. Strain and reserve. Clean fish and shred. Reserve.

The rice is best prepared in a paella pan. Heat 180ml olive oil and fry off 2 garlic cloves until golden. Remove garlic and sauté a broken in pieces dried red pepper (ñora). Place garlic and red pepper, salt and pepper, 2 tablespoons of parsley, and a pinch of saffron into a blender and buzz till finely chopped. Add a cup of the broth. Reheat the oil in the paella pan, add 2 more cloves of minced garlic and a large finely chopped tomato. Sauté for a few minutes and then add pepper mixture and five more cups of the broth, the whiting and shrimps and bring to the boil. Cook uncovered and stirring until the rice has not quite absorbed the liquid. Put in the oven about 180 deg C for about 15 minutes. Leave to stand for about 10 minutes with a piece of foil loosely covering. Serve simply with salad and apparently alioli!

Desserts

Undoubtedly the most famous desert of Alicante is Turrón, which is a type of nougat made using honey and almonds. Almonds are grown extensively all over the Valencian and Murcian regions, and the trees provide plenty of nuts!

Turrón is typically eaten around Christmas time, but available all year round in most supermarkets. The genuine brands are those from the town of Jijona (very sweet and soft) and Alicante (hard and crunchy). There is also another called *turrón a la piedra* which is crammed with crunchy almonds flavoured with grated lemon rind and cinnamon.

Since 1881 the Don Valeriano López Lloret family have been making chocolates in Villajoyosa. They have a chocolate museum with free entry. *www.valor.es*

No visit to the region would be complete without at least sampling the wares, which are widely available in all supermarkets. One of their straplines is "Over a century dedicated to the pleasure of working for pleasure." You know what they say about sex and chocolate? Well apparently in Villajoyosa, chocolate wins...

TRANSPORT

AIRPORTS

Alicante, El Altet Airport, ☎ 966 919 000

El Altet Airport (ALC) just gets bigger and bigger. It is accessed by a costal road and the motorway (A7). Taxis to Alicante town centre are about €15 - €20. To Benidorm or Altea about €65 - €80. Torrevieja, €55 - €65.

There is an air-conditioned bus just outside the airport which will take you to the train station (about a 40 minute ride) for around €1.20 - excellent value.

Murcia , San Javier, ☎ 968 172 000

The Murcia-San Javier (MJV) airport is on the coast of the Mar Menor to the south of San Pedro del Pinatar in the Costa Cálida region.

Transport from the airport is restricted to taxis and a journey to the city of Murcia will cost about €60 and to Torrevieja around €80.

The closest train station is in Balsicas. You can get a bus (latbus number 73) direct to the Murcia's bus station for €7 (although be aware that there are only 3 buses a day which are all in the evening).

www.aena.es will allow you to see live arrivals and departures for all Spanish airports, in English.

Valencia, ☎ 902 404 704

Valencia airport (VLC) is easily accessed from the national road N-220, which connects the A-3 and the N-335. It is the 8th busiest airport in Spain, with many national and international flights.

There are no trains at Valencia Airport so the easiest way of transferring is via one of the buses or by catching a Taxi which can be found directly opposite the arrivals hall.

CAR HIRE COMPANIES

Centauro, *www.centauro.net*, ☎968 572 185

Europa, *www.europa-rentacar.es*, ☎968 336 523

Europ Car, *www.europcar.es*, ☎968 335 546

Sol Mar, *www.solmar.es*, ☎968 335 542

National Atesa, *www.atesa.es*, ☎965 682 803

Auriga, *www.aurigacar.com*, ☎965 687 918

Avis, *www.avis-europe.com*, ☎965 682 779

Hertz, *www.hertz.com*, ☎966 919 125

Record Rent a Car, *www.recordrentacar.com*, ☎902 123 002

RAILWAYS

Spain's railways are part of the network *www.renfe.es*. Plans are in place for a sophisticated expansion of railway lines, intercity and international.

At the other end of the spectrum are the delightful FGV lines. The Costa Blanca Express from Alicante to Dénia. There's also the Limón Exprés (will be back in operation from the end of 2008) from Benidorm to Gata de Gorgos. For more information visit *www.fgv.es* or call ☎900 720 472

For a return ticket ask for "ida y vuelte."

As in UK, Spain has a number of companies using the network and prices vary accordingly. It is often wise to buy tickets in advance at railway stations for important journeys. Generally there is car parking at railway stations.

It is worth noting that disabled and the over 60s can buy a gold card known as a *tarjeta dorada* for €5 which lasts one year. On the fast trains, Monday to Thursday this card will get you a 40% reduction and 25% on the weekends. You will get 40% off the cost of all other trains all week. A student card receives 25% discount.

Coaches and Buses

You can just about get from anywhere to anywhere by coach and do it cheaply too. More Spanish people travel by coach than by train. An arm of National Express called ALSA are the biggest operators. You can buy tickets online (they will send you an SMS and email confirmation), at a travel agent or at the bus station. For popular routes buy your tickets in advance. *www.alsa.es*, ☎902 422 242

You can also call Estacion de Autobuses Interurbanos Alicante for timetables and information ☎965 13 0700

Ferries

From Alicante you can get to: Orán (Algeria), Ibiza and Tabarca. From Dénia to: Mallorca, Ibiza and Formentera. From Santa Pola to Tabarca. These sites will help you book your journey:

www.directferries.es
www.trasmediterranea.es
www.turismosantapola.es

CLIMATE

You can enjoy the coast practically year-round in the Alicante region from the Easter holidays and well into autumn. There are a great variety of water activities, from sailing to windsurfing to water-skiing, scuba diving and kayaking. The average temperature during the year ranges from 13°C in winter to 27°C in summer. The climate is dry, hot in summer and mild in winter.

The World Health Organisation describes the climate of the Costa Blanca as being one of the best in the world. Alicante's summers are hot but not too hot due to the cooling breezes and the winters in are mild with many clear blue sunny days. The climate and weather is very healthy especially for sufferers of arthritis.

Rain is scarce throughout the region, falling mainly in the spring (May) and autumn (October), leaving the summer wonderfully dry. However, due to geography, the temperature differences between the coast and the interior are much more extreme in the winter. On the coast temperatures tend never to fall below 10°C, while inland at higher altitudes they may not exceed 6°C.

Alicante Weather

	day avg. °C	night avg. °C	sea avg. °C	mm/ day	hours/ day
JAN	13	6	14	31	5
FEB	14	7	13	39	6
MAR	16	9	14	48	7
APR	19	11	15	43	8
MAY	21	14	17	54	9
JUN	25	18	21	37	10
JUL	27	21	21	27	11
AUG	27	21	25	49	10
SEP	25	19	24	76	8
OCT	21	15	21	86	6
NOV	16	11	18	52	5
DEC	13	8	15	45	4

ECONOMY

The economy in the Alicante region is based mainly on the services sector, data from 2005 suggested that over 84% of the active populace work in this sector.

Tourism has played an important role in the development of the city.

The economy of the Alicante region includes salt, wine, tobacco, aluminium and fishing; textiles including carpet manufacture at Crevillent; marble quarrying especially around La Romana and Novelda; shoe manufacture particularly at Elche and Elda and toy manufacture centred on Ibi.

The city of Alicante occupies the 5th slot in level of commercial importance in Spain (beaten by Madrid, Barcelona, Valencia and Seville).

The University of Alicante, in San Vicente del Raspeig, has more than 33,000 students and attracts an important number of foreign students. The university accounts for over 6% of the active populace.

The Port of Alicante is in a phase of expansion. At the moment, more than 15,000 people work directly or indirectly in these facilities. Historically, the Port of Alicante has been intimately bound to the destiny of the city. It will be interesting to see how this develops.

There is also the film studio La Ciudad de la Luz which made "Asterix and the Olympic Games". With 26 productions filmed (at the time of writing) La Ciudad de la Luz studios has brought in 249 million euro, with a direct investment of around 85 million euro into the region. These productions have lead to some 114,130 overnight stays in hotels across the region over the last three years. *www.ciudaddelaluz.com*

GOING NATIVE IN ALICANTE

Many books have been written to help people who are moving to or have recently arrived in Spain – Yolanda Solo's *'Spain: The Expat Survival Guide'* also published by NativeSpain is a good example. The following tips, however, have been adapted from advice given by Simon Harris in his book - *'Going Native in Catalonia'*.

Successful long-term residents...

- ...are adaptable and tolerant. This means that the initial culture shock and different way of doing things can be taken on with ease.

- ...are individualistic and independent. Not hanging out with people who are the same as you allows you to make your own way in a new culture. You need to be able to enjoy difference and diversity while retaining a strong sense of your own identity.

- ...are good language learners. If you haven't already got at least an 'A' level in French or Spanish, you will need to apply yourself to learning Spanish with commitment and enthusiasm. To really fit in and 'go native' you may wish to become familiar with Valencian (similar to, but not the same as, Catalan) too.

- ...are thick-skinned but open-minded. Foreign tourists get ripped off and occasionally insulted in every country in the world. Bad experiences should be water off a duck's back, so don't trick yourself into believing that everybody shares the opinions of the occasional racist.

- ...make flexible plans. Amongst the successful long-term residents I know the reasons for coming here in the first place are extremely diverse; a post-MA exchange programme, to practise the language after completing a Spanish degree, to become a professional flamenco dancer or, in my case, because I was offered a free place to stay for a few months. If asked, most of us will tell you that we stayed because we liked it, life events seemed to be telling us that this was the place to be, and that if we'd had any regrets we would have moved on.

- ...have emotional ties in Spain. Whether these be friends, partners or children, after a while it's important to have the people you love most close to you. There are people I miss back home but it's impossible for me to see my wife (who I met here) and daughter as foreigners.

- ...maximise their skills in two directions. Whether you're an engineer, a dentist or a rock musician, the knowledge you bring with you is an important selling point. Once you've learned how things work in Spain you have insider information that is saleable back home. A simple example is teaching English language and culture to the locals and then writing about my new home for the English-speaking market!

- ...'Think Positive'. However long you stay, there'll be good days and bad days. The trick is to focus on what you like about being here. In my case, this is the light; so being able to have breakfast in bright (but cold) sunshine on my terrace in mid-January is a great cure for any ills.

Not everybody wants to spend the rest of their life away from their home country. A short stay of a few months to a couple of years can be fulfilling and rewarding and will be an experience that will stay with you forever. However, there are certain people that from day one seem doomed to fail – you can normally spot them a mile away and I suggest you avoid them like the plague.

- People who are continually criticising life back home. They arrive rubbishing everything they've left behind. Within a few months they'll be rubbishing the life they've built around themselves.

- People who are running away from something. Some shady characters go to live in far-flung lands, but a more common example is couples who think a change of air might sort things out between them. Often it just exacerbates underlying problems and brings them out into the open.

- People who assume everything's going to be the same as it was back home. You're going to have to adapt to a new lifestyle. You're going to have to learn a new language. Most of your assumptions about how things should be done are going to be challenged. If you're not prepared to take this on board, you're better off staying at home.

- People who are constantly homesick. I also miss so many tangible and intangible things, but if things were so great back home, why did you leave in the first place?

People with no money. Not only are they irritating sponges who don't bother to find a local source of income before it's too late, but they'll be running back home soon (probably owing you a few Euros!)

So what is the key to making a successful move?

This obviously depends on your age and the degree to which you wish to integrate, but know this before you go, and get some experience before you burn your boats.

Younger people (18-40)

If you are young(ish) and still in a position to decide where your life wants to go, there are a number of options open to you.

- Undergraduates. The ERASMUS programme (*www.erasmus.ac.uk*), which has operated since 1987, gives students the chance to spend 3 to 12 months in a foreign country continuing their education and gaining all-important credits. Exchanges are usually organised by the home university, so everything is set up before you leave.

- Postgraduates. Don't underestimate the broad range of courses on offer for Master's degrees and the excellent level of tutoring for doctoral theses in Spain. You would be mad to even think about it without a competent level of Spanish.

- English Teaching. Long gone are the days when you could turn up and get a job just because you spoke English. You will need a CELTA (the basic teaching certificate available through Cambridge TESOL) or the Trinity equivalent, which can be obtained in the UK and, once qualified, you'll be able to apply for jobs in the educational supplements of the British broadsheets.

- A Proper Job. If you work for an international company with offices in Alicante, you could join the increasing number of workers who take advantage of a secondment abroad. Your company's Human Resources department should be able to organise everything for you. If you're looking for a new job then sites such as *www.empleo.net, www.faster.es, www.Infoempleo.com, www.jobtoasterspain.com, www.laborman.es, www.miltrabajos.com, www.monster.es, www.recruitspain.com, www.trabajar.com and www.trabajos.com* are worth your time. Bear in mind, though, that a move might also involve a drop in salary.

Older People (35-70+)

Whilst many people will always come to Alicante to spend their retirement, this group has been joined by an increasing number of young professionals who, often as a result of the Internet, are able to continue their career in sunnier climes. If you belong to one of these groups, you will have an independent income. But even so making Alicante your permanent home requires a great deal of thought, planning and research.

A Research Visit

If, during your wild and reckless youth, you did some travelling and these travels brought you to Spain for a period of time, then you'll know the score (things have changed superficially in the last 20 years, but the essence of everything remains the same). However, if you fell in love with the place whilst here on holiday, you would be foolish not to get an idea of what it's like to live here all year round.

A short stay of a few months to a couple of years can be fulfilling and rewarding and will be an experience that will stay with you forever.

You could plan a number of short trips at different times of the year, but if I were you I'd commit myself to something a little longer. A visit that would give you time to learn about, reflect on and possibly prepare a future permanent move – a short section in a book like this cannot do that for you.

This should be done out of season, as particularly on the coast and the more touristy areas, renting will be a lot cheaper. You'll have the chance to see what life is like when all the crowds have gone away. Your favourite restaurant may be closed. British newspapers won't be on sale. You may have to get in the car just to do your basic shopping. Furthermore, you'll find that nobody speaks English anymore so, if you still like it, this may be the time to take that language course that you'd always meant to take but never got round to.

Where are you going to live?

- Provincial Capitals or Small Towns. Property bargains can still be found. Depending where you go, you might get by with only a basic level of Spanish but in many towns (particularly inland) you'll find yourself a little cut-off unless you learn Spanish and Valencian.

- Villages and Rural Isolation. If you go inland, you can still find reasonably priced properties in idyllic settings, but these will often require quite a lot of work. You have to be clear how much you can do yourself and how much you're prepared to pay to have the house of your dreams. You should also remember that rural isolation can be very, well, *isolated* and even the most basic facilities will probably be a drive away. This may be just what you want when you're young and fit but might become more of a problem, as you get increasingly dependent on health care, for example.

- Urbanisations. These housing estates normally provide individual houses built on a plot of land. Often situated within easy reach of the coast, they are home to a mix of locals and foreigners, who may live there permanently or use them as holiday homes. Prices vary depending on the size of the property and the number of communal facilities, and you may see homes advertised 'off plan' (you buy the property before it has been built). There are a number of risks involved in the latter option, as you often don't know exactly when the urbanisation will be finished, what it will look like when it is or what the community atmosphere will be like.

- Costa Communities. Torrevieja, Alicante, Benidorm and other cities on the coast may suit people who want to live in Spain but aren't necessarily planning on 'going native' in the full sense of the word. Here, more people will speak English and you'll find plenty of expats. However, out of season that delightfully bustling summer town might become completely deserted, and when there are no customers most, if not all, the shops, bars and restaurants will close down too.

BUYING IN ALICANTE - AT-A-GLANCE

To give the subject of buying property in Alicante the attention it deserves would require a whole book but to point you in the right direction Debbie Jenkins, author of *'Buying Property in Murcia'* and *'Going Native in Murcia'*, has laid out the main steps to take on the following pages.

The 2 golden rules when buying property in Spain are 1) always do your research and 2) employ a qualified professional.

For more information, facts, advice and books on buying property in Spain visit Debbie's blog at *www.spanishpropertyexpert.com*

Decide Why You're Buying

☐ Investment
☐ Rental
☐ Holidays
☐ For Family
☐ To Live

⬇

Determine Budget

☐ Mortgage/remortgage
☐ Staged financing
☐ Credit Cards
☐ Sell something/cash in stocks or options
☐ Get Financial Advice

⬇

Do Research

☐ Internet – look up estate agents, abogados, gestors, architects etc
☐ Decide which towns to shortlist
☐ Check the latest at *www.spanishpropertyexpert.com*
☐ Recommendations – from friends, bulletin boards, magazines

⬇

Make Criteria

Where? ☐town ☐village ☐seaside ☐mountains ☐countryside ☐urbanisation
Transport? ☐driving ☐trains ☐airports ☐motorways
Amenities? ☐hospitals ☐schools ☐colleges ☐nightlife ☐restaurants & bars
Type? ☐restoration ☐new build ☐off plan ☐pre-owned

⬇

Make Specification

Size? ☐bedrooms ☐bathrooms ☐garage
Outdoor space? ☐garden ☐patio ☐pool ☐trees

⬇

Arrange Research Trip

☐ Flights
☐ Accommodation
☐ Travel
☐ Meetings – Agent, Abogado, Gestor, Architect etc.

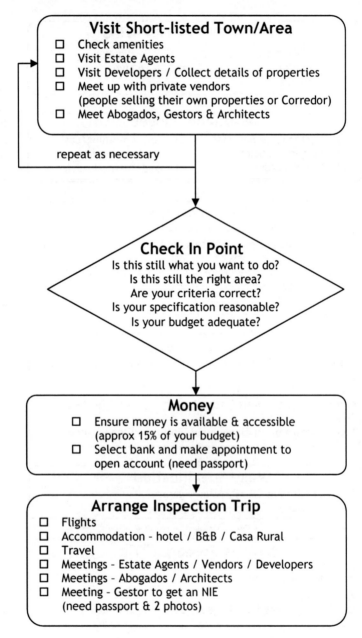

Visit Short-listed Town/Area
- ☐ Check amenities
- ☐ Visit Estate Agents
- ☐ Visit Developers / Collect details of properties
- ☐ Meet up with private vendors
  (people selling their own properties or Corredor)
- ☐ Meet Abogados, Gestors & Architects

repeat as necessary

Check In Point
Is this still what you want to do?
Is this still the right area?
Are your criteria correct?
Is your specification reasonable?
Is your budget adequate?

Money
- ☐ Ensure money is available & accessible
  (approx 15% of your budget)
- ☐ Select bank and make appointment to
  open account (need passport)

Arrange Inspection Trip
- ☐ Flights
- ☐ Accommodation – hotel / B&B / Casa Rural
- ☐ Travel
- ☐ Meetings – Estate Agents / Vendors / Developers
- ☐ Meetings – Abogados / Architects
- ☐ Meeting – Gestor to get an NIE
  (need passport & 2 photos)

Step 2: In Spain - Research Trip

Step 3: At Home - Organise Inspection Trip

Accompanied Viewings

- ☐ Be clear on criteria
- ☐ Be flexible
- ☐ Take camera and video camera – take lots of photos and video footage to help decide later
- ☐ Take GPS coordinates
- ☐ Make notes

Make Short List

- ☐ Compare each property against original criteria
- ☐ Deselect any obvious properties
- ☐ Revisit properties alone – use the GPS coordinates!
- ☐ Meet with neighbours
- ☐ Check out local amenities
- ☐ Discuss with Abogado – is the paperwork correct, are they able to sell it, is it what & where you thought it was, does the nota simple look right?
- ☐ Discuss with Architect – can you do renovations, building works, is it architecturally sound, what are the likely costs involved?

Check In Point

Is this still what you want to do?
Is this still the right area?
Are your criteria correct?
Is your specification reasonable?
Is your budget adequate?

Choose Property

- ☐ Make offer
- ☐ Sign contract
- ☐ Give deposit – usually 10%
- ☐ Set up bank account – Gestor can help
- ☐ Set up Post Office box for correspondence
- ☐ Organise NIE – Gestor can do this
- ☐ Select Abogado – choose an English-speaking solicitor and instruct them

Get Money
- ☐ Make arrangements to acquire the necessary money
- ☐ Transfer money to bank account in Spain

Wait
- ☐ Abogado will tell you when paperwork is ready

Arrange Buying Trip
- ☐ Flights
- ☐ Accommodation – hotel / B&B / Casa Rural
- ☐ Travel

Completion
- ☐ Visit Abogado agent who will tell you plans
- ☐ Go to bank and order money – probably cheque and cash
- ☐ Go to bank and withdraw cash and get cheque
- ☐ Notario appointment (usually arranged by Abogado)
- ☐ Read through all documents in presence of Notario & sellers
- ☐ Hand over cheque
- ☐ Sign LOTS of documents
- ☐ Receive keys – congratulations, you've finalised your property purchase

Receive Deeds (Escritura)
- ☐ 6–12 months after purchase

Step 5: At Home – Get Money

Step 6: In Spain – Finalise Purchase

Town and City Guides

Many of the tourist offices for the towns have websites. I have included them where possible along with a telephone number. Some of the websites are excellent, providing a wealth of information in many languages including English. Others are, shall I say, "interesting"!

According to the figures of 2008, Alicante province still has the highest number of blue flags awarded (for beaches and marinas) in Spain. Even the blue flags themselves are recyclable. They are "binned" appropriately at the end of the year.

THE COMARCAS

I've broken the next section down into the 9 Comarcas of Alicante as indicated on this map.

MARINA ALTA

Benissa

Benissa is just an hour away from Alicante airport, with a population of 9000. It's one of the oldest towns on the Costa Blanca, lying just inland to the north of Benidorm. It boasts 4km of interesting coastline including white sandy beaches, rocky coves and cliff tops within easy reach. Benissa's well preserved medieval town centre with its churches, fine houses, ironwork balconies and narrow winding streets is also home to *The Palacio de los Torres-Orduña* originally owned by the Lords of Guadelest now open to the public as a library and cultural centre.

Sometimes known as "little Europe" due to the large number of northern Europeans who make their home here it is much quieter than the nearby Benidorm and appeals to couples.

Fiestas include the Moors and Christians at the end of June, and the fiesta patronal on the 4th Sunday in April, where bulls, parties and fireworks play their part.

All of Benissa's beaches have crystal clear water revealing the marvellous, rocky seabeds so appreciated by diving and sailing enthusiasts. The busiest one of all is Fustera cove. It has the greater number of facilities in addition to sports and children's recreation areas. A small marina located on the Calpe boundary has a sailing school and diving centre.

A peaceful town with white houses and narrow, deserted streets, Benissa is an enjoyable place to visit. It has a lovely white church, known as the 'Cathedral of the Marina Alta' and the old prison serves as a youth centre. The main town is located on the side of a mountain and there are some beautiful views down to Calpe and its magnificent rock.

Benissa is a service centre of sorts for the villages inland. It currently has 4 large supermarkets, DIY stores and shops selling English products.

A fresh produce market is held in the main square on Tuesdays and there is a flea market on a Thursday. Benissa is easily accessible, situated right next to the motorway.

Restaurante Casa Canto, Avenida Paix Valencia 237, T: 965 730 629 for fish dishes and paella de Benissa.

The Sierra Bernia nature park is absolutely great for hiking and rock climbing. The bus that serves the inland villages leaves from Benissa. Ifach Golf Club is 4km away.

Close to Benissa, separated only by the A-7 motorway, lies the village of **Senija** with a population of 470. Situated at the foot of a small mountain, it is a little village with numerous English urbanizations. There is one shop and two bars but no restaurants.

<u>Places To Stay</u>
Cases de Sant Jaume ★★★ T: 966 499 075, *www.hotelcasesdesantjaume.com*

Al Zaraq, T: 965 731 615, *www.alzaraq.net*

Casa Rural Dolores, T: 965 731 573

Casa El Peón de Pinos, T: 965 731 573

Tourist Information

www.benissa.net, T: 965 732 225

Calpe (Calp)

Many years ago it was a sleepy little fishing village but for better or worse it is now a mini Benidorm.

Calpe is a coastal town located 67km north of Alicante at the foot of the Natural Park of *Peñón de Ifach* (Ifach Rock). The economy is based solidly on tourism and fishing with a strong British contingent.

The impressive rock called *Peñón de Ifach* that overlooks Calpe is a major draw to visitors who get a spectacular view of the local bays and town from its summit.

Tourist attractions worth visiting in Calpe are the ruins of *Los baños de la Reina* (the queen's baths), the bird sanctuary on the flooded salt flats and the 18th century tower of *La Peça*.

There's a modern marina, old fishing port and several nautical clubs. The two main fine sandy beaches are the Playas Arenal and Cantal Roig.

The area is popular with climbers. The massive limestone outcrop is the tallest rock in the entire Mediterranean and it splits Calpe's shoreline in two. The rock has been designated as a Natural Park and its summit offers fantastic views of the Costa Blanca. Calpe boasts 11km of clean, sandy beaches with several coves suitable for snorkelling and fishing. Enticingly it has a freshwater cave, *Cueva dels Coloms*, only accessible from the sea.

The market is held on a Saturday and a flea market each Wednesday.

Being a major tourist destination it offers a wide range of hotels, bars and shops and because of the fishing port you can expect its restaurants to offer an excellent selection of fresh, locally caught seafood.

Easy to reach from Alicante as it is situated 10km off the motorway north of Altea.

The Club de Golf Ifach is 4km outside Calpe.

Places To Stay
Bahía Calpe ★★★★ T: 965 839 702, *www.torsehoteles.com*

Gran Hotel Sol y Mar ★★★★ T: 965 875 055

Diamante Beach ★★★★ T: 965 875 609

SH Ifach ★★★★ T: 965 874 500

Roca Esmeralda ★★★ T: 965 836 101

Porto Calpe ★★ T: 965 837 322, *www.portocalpe.com*

Galetamar, T: 965 832 311

Tourist Information
www.calpe.es, T: 965 838 532

Castell de Castells

Castell de Castells is a small village at the source of the Río Jalón in a mountainous area. Clearly a place for walkers and lovers of culture. Reading the programme of events as I write for this town I note that it is to have a Week of Culture with poetry readings at the *Font d'la Bota*, music concerts in the square, performed by the village band "*La Primitiva*", traditional dancing with entertainment for young and old and a Gastronomic Fair/Fare.

San Vicente Ferrer is celebrated at Easter time while Santa Ana is the patron saint of Castell de Castells. July 26th is fiesta day, a time of great celebration in the village with a candlelit procession through the streets in the evening.

Three kilometres outside this village is *Els Arcs*, a natural arch.

Places To Stay
Serrella, T: 965 518 138

Casa Rural Pilar, T: 965 518 517

Tourist Information
www.castelldecastells.es, T: 965 518 067

Dénia

Dénia, dedicated by the Romans to Diana the Huntress is a small town of approximately 44,000 located in the north of Alicante. Its coastal location proves popular with tourists and the population doubles during the summer months. Dénia also provides ferries to the Balearic islands of Ibiza and Mallorca and also Formentera.

Huge quantities of raisins were exported from here in the past. The Dénia grapes were dried off the vine in a process completed in just a few days. This allowed the raisins to be exported to the UK ahead of the superior Malaga raisins which were dried on the vine.

With a huge range of places to visit there is much to keep anyone busy. Its streets are a fascinating showcase of architecture through the ages. The 16th century castle which dominates the town is a good starting point.

The fishing quarters of Baix La Marand Les Roques retain their intimate Spanish charm and the 17th century church of Santa María is outstanding. With 20kms of seafront, Dénia has enough sand and space to keep everyone happy. There are different beaches to suit everyone - endless stretches of flat sandy beach, rocky coves and tiny bays hidden among the cliffs.

The town has a beautiful main street lined with trees whose branches dip towards one another, forming a natural arch. It is closed off to vehicles in the evenings so that all can enjoy a leisurely, peaceful stroll. From the castle and from the tower 6km from Dénia, the Torre del Gerro, you can enjoy some superb views of Dénia and her surroundings.

Dénia is heavily developed, it is extremely popular with northern European tourists, particularly Germans.

Dénia's main attraction is its varied 20km coastline which is made up of a sandy beach (to the north), the harbour and a rocky beach, which is a haven for scuba and snorkelling enthusiasts. You will often see people diving from the rocky beach at La Punta Negra or at the huge cliff near the end of Les Rotes.

While the town is full of tourist apartments Dénia still retains much of its old charm. A walk through the old fisherman's quarter, the harbour and main street (*Carrer Marqués de Campos*) will give you a taste of real Spain.

Dénia was the capital of the Moorish Taifa kingdom in the 11th and 12th centuries which extended to Alicante, parts of Murcia and the Balearic Islands. The castle dates from this period and dominates much of the town. It has many later additions including the Governor's Palace (*Palau del Governador*) which houses the archaeological museum. The castle is also well worth a visit for its views alone. Access is on foot by steps near the town hall or by little train from near the tourist office or you can drive up. It is quite well sign-posted.

The Ayuntamiento (town hall) has two Roman memorial tablets set in the wall, recovered from the Ancient Temple of Diana.

The very good toy museum reflects the opening of the first factory in Dénia in 1904 making tin-plate toys with machinery and models from Germany. Another factory opened making wooden toys and this became Dénia's trademark. The museum is on the first floor of the art centre in the old station building and entrance is free.

Dénia is also good for pottering around the colourful streets behind the promenade and there are lots of restaurants. Get great ice cream at Tutto Fruto on Esplanada Cervantes or Heladeria Verdu on Marquès de Campo. Further up Marquès de Campo, try Tasca Euladia for coffee, beer and tapas. Quality retail therapy opportunities abound.

Fiestas in Dénia include the popular fiesta Fallas in March where huge papier-mâché statues (fallas) are set ablaze.

La Sella Golf Club is on the outskirts of Dénia. There are four other golf courses all within a twenty minute drive from Dénia.

Just up the coast from Dénia, **Els Poblets** is almost an extension of the main town. It is very popular with English and German tourists and expatriates and has plenty of villas. There is apparently a "Craft Fair" at Els Poblet, between Vergel and Dénia. There is one supermarket in the village, complete with bar inside.

Cabezo de Oro, "the big golden head" is said to be the perfect place to climb in the summer as it is in shade until 3pm.

The tourist office is very near the station on the way to the esplanade. You can book boat trips and tourist trains round the town from another office a few metres away. The only train, affectionately referred to as the Limón Exprés, into Dénia travels through mountains and along the coast from Alicante. The picturesque 2.5 hour journey provides passengers with an interesting sightseeing trip. At the time of writing this service had been suspended for major renovations and is due to re-open at the end of 2008.

Places To Stay
Denia Marriott La Sella Golf Resort & Spa ★★★★★
T: 966 454 054

Buenavista ★★★★ T: 965 787 995, *www.buenavistadenia.com*

Noguera Mar Hotel ★★★ T: 966 475 650, *www.nogueramarhotel.com*

Port Denia ★★★ T: 965 781 212, *www.onasol.es*
Romano, ★★★ T: 966 421 789

Castillo ★ T: 966 435 260

L'Anfora, T: 966 430 101, *www.hostallanfora.com*

Daniya Spa & Business, T: 902 364 041

Comercio, T: 965 780 071

Tourist Information
www.denia.net, T: 966 422 367

Gata de Gorgos
This little town near Dénia is on the N-332 and is the cradle of basketry. If you want anything in wicker or grass then visit here. The area surrounding it grows almonds and muscatel grapes so it's also a good place to buy these products.

Places To Stay
Avenida ★ T: 965 626 333

Nou Avenida, T: 966 454 434, *www.hotelnouavenida.com*

The Jalón Valley and Jalón
The valley between the inland mountains of La Marina Alta is rich in orange and almond groves and has numerous vineyards. The area is scattered with some lovely villages where people seeking refuge from the

busy coastal areas have chosen to buy property. Most of the villages have an expatriate population and some have English bars. The area attracts more foreign residents than foreign tourists, who tend to stick to the coast. A famous wine growing region, the natives of the villages speak Valenciano rather than Spanish.

There are 2 buses a day that start at Dénia and finish at Castell de Castells, serving the whole area.

The main village of the area, Jalón is noted for its bodegas that offer excellent wine at very low prices. It is a beautiful village, in an enviable rural setting, stretched out over a valley floor. Its church roof is notable for its amazing mirrored tiles. The mountainsides around the village are fast becoming burnt out and built on, as Jalón continues to attract foreign residents who outnumber the Spanish natives.

Jalón's fiesta in August is a chaotic, frenzied affair. As in the other villages of the area, bull-running takes place through the streets and cages are set up where people climb inside whilst the bulls butt the cages. Well-known Spanish bands play on the stage and fireworks with the accompanying firework fights are popular.

Jalón's "rastro" (flea market) is worth a visit. It takes place on a Sunday and market stalls stretch for 2km down a dry riverbed. The food market is held on a Wednesday.

English people can feel at home as there is a fish and chip shop, an English bar called "Bully's Bar", English clothes shops and restaurants.

Jalón is 15km from the sea and 5km from Benissa. Alicante is 80km away and Valencia 91km. Ifach Golf Club is 11km away.

There are numerous villages scattered around Jalón in the valley, all set in rural surroundings.

Jalón is their main small service centre and the larger coastal towns are within easy reach, less than 20km away.

2km away from Jalón, **Alcalalí** is a small Spanish village in the heart of the Pop valley halfway between Jalón and Parcent. It was originally a Moorish farmstead and the village is surrounded by vineyards and orange, almond and olive groves.

Many English people live in Alcalalí and about 30% of children in the school there are foreign nationals. Alcalalí has a few small shops including a butchers and a tobacconist, 3 Spanish bars, an English bar and a German bar.

At the foot of the Sierra del Recingle, near to Orba, is the little village of Tormos with its excellent Spanish restaurant.

Just west of Orba is the village of **Benidoleig**. At the foot of the Sierra de Seguili in the heart of the Marina Alta, Bendioleig is a farming community with a population of 783. Steep, winding streets lead through the village, which is surrounded by almond and olive trees. Benidoleig is famous for its *Cueva de Calaveras* – the cave of skulls, where 12 skulls were discovered in the 18th century. The skulls were the remains of Moorish explorers who had died whilst investigating the caves. Remains dating back to Neolithic times have also been discovered there.

Benidoleig is easily accessible, being just 4km from the A-7 motorway.

The tiny village of **Murla** with 330 inhabitants is west of Alcalalí. A game called *pelota valenciana* originates from here, which is a handball game, played by two teams using their bare hands to bat a calfskin ball over a cord. Huge amounts of money may be won or lost as betting is part of the game! The locals who play matches at weekends consider this game very important. So much so that the main square is named after one of its best pelota players.

Backed by a mountain, the village has an unusual fortified church with illuminated crypts and reconstructed towers. There is 1 small shop, and a fruit and vegetable market in the village square. The village is fairly isolated, not being on the bus route. It is a 3km walk to the nearest bus stop.

South of Alcalalí and Murla, the village of **Parcent** is a small place surrounded by orange, almond and olive groves with a church at its centre. Its steep, pretty streets and its beautiful surroundings have earned it the name of "paradise between the mountains". There is evidence of its importance as a grape growing centre in the form of old raisin driers that can be seen around the village although today, most villagers work on the coast.

The main medical centre of the area is in Parcent.

There are a few bars and restaurants. Parcent boasts the best paella restaurant in the area.

West of Parcent is **Benichembla**, a village with one of the lowest altitudes of the villages in the Alicante province, located next to the Gorgos river. The inhabitants have traditionally practiced "valley" agriculture where vines and citrus fruits are grown and the grapes left to dry in the ancient rius-raus – drying houses, where they turn into raisins. A lovely little village with a population of 400, there is a fresh water spring with a fountain and a lavadera where old women can still be seen washing their clothes. The church there has a pleasant interior.

Benichembla has 2 good bars and a decent restaurant.

Places To Stay

Casa Julia ★★★★ T: 966 405 050

Casa Regina, T: 966 405 038

Casa Barranco, T: 966 480 346

Tourist Information

www.valldepop.es, T: 966 482 024

Jávea (Xábia)

Jávea is midway between Valencia to the north and Alicante to the south. Protected from harsh winter winds of the north by Montgó, it enjoys a unique micro-climate that the World Health Organisation says makes it one of the healthiest places in the world.

There are more recorded hours of sunshine per year in Jávea than in any other place in Spain, making it a popular place for affluent northern Europeans to buy property. As well as tourists from overseas many Spaniards come to Jávea, the busiest period being during August, when the population swells to over 100,000.

Jávea is made up of the old town, the port and the beach area of Arenal. The old town is a maze of narrow winding streets with ancient churches and houses with wrought iron balconies and gothic-style windows. The harbour and fishing port have numerous restaurants and bars serving delicious fresh-caught fish and overlooking the Mediterranean sea. The Arenal beach area is where to find most of the shops, bars and restaurants.

This is a relaxing town offering many museums, weekly open-air markets and spectacular views of the area from nearby Montgó.

Their Moors and Christians fiesta is celebrated between the 16th and 20th July. Their fiesta patronal, *Nuestra Señora de Loreto*, with the bull-running on the harbour walls and a firework display is celebrated in September.

Nuestra Senora de Loreto is a modern church, its design imitating the keel of a ship.

If you enjoy scuba diving experience the *Cueva de Agua Dulce* (the freshwater cave) with its two lakes, *Els Orgues* and *del Aiguadolç*, situated just north of Jávea, on the coast close to *Cabo de la Nao*.

Probably the largest cemetery in the province (part of which is rumoured to lie under the Alkazaba holiday apartments) can also be found in the town and in the 1990's, the police station (then part of the Ayuntamiento) was moved to a purpose-built location in order to open a tourist office in its original home. But, when builders began work on relaying the floor they discovered fourteenth century graves (complete with skeletons!). Today several of the rock-cut graves (without their skeletal inmates) have been preserved and can be seen under a glass floor.

The imposing limestone mountain (Montgó) rises up 750m from the plain just a few hundred metres from the sea and almost parallel to the coastline between Jávea and neighbouring Dénia. Montgó is home to over 600 different species of plants, some of which are unique to this area. You can climb to the top of Montgó from all sides, which is an enjoyable journey through a varied landscape of croplands, pine forests, scrubland and rocky areas with caves (with ancient cave paintings in Migdia cave). The summit offers breathtaking panoramic views of the surrounding area and the island of Ibiza can be seen on a clear day.

Jávea has all the amenities you could need from hotels to villas and supermarkets to discos and golf (Club de Golf Javea) is easily accessible from the A-7.

A weekly street market is held in the old town on Thursdays.

Paradores are state run hotels. There is only one in the province which is at Jávea. Rated as four stars it is situated in Arenal, Javea, 90 kilometres from Alicante and 112 kilometres from Valencia.

Places To Stay

Parador de Jávea, T: 965 790 200, *www.parador.es*

Rodat Village & Spa ★★★★ T: 966 470 710, *www.elrodat.com*

Villa Naranjos ★★ T: 965 790 050, *www.villanaranjos.com*

Triskel, T: 966 462 191

Roig 53, T: 966 461 787

Solymar, T: 966 461 919

Costa Mar, T: 965 790 644

Tourist Information

www.xabia.org, T: 965 794 356

Gaile Griffin Peers on Jávea

Jávea has four faces each with its own set of hybrid moods and seasonal expressions. The first three are its split personalities – the Old Town, The Port and the Arenal – the fourth is the overwhelming good nature of its inhabitants, in the "face" of every adversity thrown in their path.

The Old Town is just starting to open up again after several years of road works and town centre improvements, the businesses that have survived the renovation process are keen to welcome both their old customers and new. Shops have been restocked and restaurants redecorated, even the Post Office has had its front made more accessible. The new basement car park below the Plaza del Constitución is open, with the first half hour free to all, giving easy access for the fleet of foot who know what and where they are going! Local shop owners have clubbed together to offer free parking and are organising a series of events for 2009 when the "New" Old Town is finally open again for cars as well as business.

The Port has been under threat of modernisation for a while, but has so far resisted, feeling that it is quite busy enough, with its many and varied restaurants opening out onto the Mediterranean, pretty Marina and active fishing port.

The Arenal is the clubs and pubs area of town, but boasts many inexpensive restaurants and a wide range of cocktail bars and pleasant lunchtime Tapas spots.

If you are hungry, walk a few yards virtually anywhere in Jávea (particularly in the Port and the Arenal) and the delicious smells from its many doors will draw you in to some delightful small and friendly restaurants. For a meal 'a deux' I would definitely recommend 'Chez

Angel' near Humpty Dumpty on the Arenal inner road, not the cheapest but consistently good.

The Arenal is popular with swimmers, but if you have a sense of adventure or want to go sub aqua, go to one of the several diving centres (I use Jávea Divers next to the Tennis Club) and really enjoy Jávea's stunning underwater views. Grenadella and the Marine Reserve at Cap San Antonio are both worth the visit. In the Spring and Autumn, locals surf the waves between the Arenal and the Port.

The Montgó National Park has several listed walks – but there are many more in this area that are worth the effort and the views are gorgeous if you can take the height. Cap San Antonio is probably easier and more accessible than Cabo de la Nao. Both are stunning areas.

The Indoor market is open in the town centre and has meat and vegetables of a generally high standard, not to mention the fresh fish. Thursday is the weekly open market and is on the way to the Arenal, in the area also used for the Bull runs!

Gaile Griffin Peers
www.javeaphotos.com
www.mabusinessclub.com

Moraira

With 8km of unspoilt coast and nearby mountains the population of Moraira triples in summer. Many expats make their home here and it is a very popular retirement spot and quite an exclusive holiday resort area. As well as fishing Moraira is also famous for its Muscatel grapes used for wine making.

The small harbour houses the fish market (Lonja) which is held daily from Tuesday to Sunday. The fine marina is the home of the Moraira Club Nautico opened in 1985.

Two of the beaches of Moraira carry blue flag status and are clean, well looked after and safe for families. There are also water sports facilities available including sailing, diving, jet-skiing and water-skiing. A weekly market is held every Friday next to the main beach, selling fresh produce, clothes and gifts.

In July the Virgin of the Unsheltered and the Virgin of Carmen (who is said to protect the sailors and fishermen) are celebrated with a fiesta on the 15th and 16th of July. There is a beautiful parade and fireworks and a water procession with the statue of the Virgin floating among endless bouquets of flowers. And of course there's the Moors and Christians held between the 14th and 20th June.

Moraira also boasts one of the best restaurants in Spain the award winning Girasol is reputedly the best restaurant on the Costa Blanca.
www.restaurantegirasol.com T: 965 744 373

Nearby Teulada is a little way inland from Moraira and here is the Bodega Cooperativa San Vicente Ferrer near the church where you can taste (and of course buy) the famous Spanish Muscatel.

Tourist Information
www.teulada-moraira.es, T: 965 745 168

Ondara

Ondara lies in the north east of the Marina Alta. The tower of the ancient Moorish castle was totally renovated in 1994 and declared an historic monument in 1996. It houses a huge clock from the beginning of the 20th century. In the *Plaza del Claustro* there are cloisters which were the former church of a convent and is now part of the town hall building. You can find a portrait of the *Mare de Deu de la Soldad*, the town's patron saint there. Ondara celebrates its fiesta in the second week of July.

Places To Stay
Ramis ★ T: 965766313

Tourist Information
www.ondara.org, T: 965 766 000

Orba

Orba is an Arabic name meaning "place where the water springs from the mountain". An important communications route, with a population of 1600, it is an attractive village in rural surroundings, citrus fruits are grown in the countryside around. The village is popular with German and English expatriates. The main school serving the surrounding area is situated here.

Next to Orba, the village of Orbeta has a large urbanization largely occupied by English expatriates.

Orba has several restaurants and bars including an English one, an English shop and an excellent pizzeria.

A public swimming pool opens in the summer months.

Orba is on the main bus route that serves the area and is 12km inland from Villajoyosa and 10km from the A-7 motorway. Alicante is 38km away on fast main roads.

The nearest golf club is Don Cayo, 13km north of Benidorm.

The villages around Orba have a less frenetic pace than their coastal counterparts. Mostly of Moorish origin, these mountain villages set in rural areas often attract foreign residents wishing to find a quieter style of life. Some of the villages, just a few kilometres away from the most visited coast in Europe, still remain relatively undiscovered.

Places To Stay
Plaça, T: 965 583 380, *www.orbahostalplaza.com*

Casa Rural Carrebaix de Orba, T: 625 139 900

Tourist Information
www.orba.es, T: 965 563 001

Teulada

Teulada used to be a walled village located slightly away from the coast for fear of attack from Berber pirates. Its proximity to the coast means that tourism is the main focus. Located on the side of the mountain with fantastic views of the coast, Teulada is a large village with a population of 10,000, attracting a number of foreign residents.

There are English, French and Russian shops in the village, reflecting its multinational population. Javea and Ifach Golf Clubs are both about 8km away.

A street market is held on Thursdays and a large flea market is held by the petrol station on Sundays.

Places To Stay
La Sort ★ ★ ★ T: 966 491 949, *www.lasort.com*

Villa Comodín, T: 965 745 834

Los Limoneros, T: 966 490 351, *www.loslimoneros.com*

Swiss Moraira, T: 965 747 104, *www.swisshotelmoraira.com*

La Marina Youth Hostel, T: 966 492 030, *www.ivaj.es*

Tourist Information
www.teulada-moraira.es, T: 965 745 168

CASE STUDY
Gaile Griffin Peers from the
UK via Cyprus, now living in Jávea
www.javeaphotos.com
www.mabusinessclub.com

When I came here I left behind one son in Cyprus and another in the UK - you put them down for a minute and the next thing you know they have taken root and don't want to move! Having lived in Cyprus for three years I couldn't bear the thought of living away from the Mediterranean and as my family had been in Jávea for the last 20 years it just seemed sensible.

I live in a villa on the foothills of the Montgó and breakfast looking inland across the valley towards Vals. Our neighbours are delightful and friendly. Its quiet, has great views and is on the edge of a National Park

I run Marina Alta Business Club. I want to bring as many of the English Speaking businesses in Marina Alta together as I can. I want those businesses to prosper, to network and to build on the good things that we as expatriates regardless of nationality, bring to this part of Spain.

My advice to people coming over is to come and talk to me and lets work together. Business Networking can be an important part of the stability and survival of small businesses.

It's very important to be able to speak Spanish. Not learning it, or at least trying is insulting our hosts, who we then oblige to learn English, Dutch, German, French etc - just because we are too lazy to learn Spanish... Having said all that, my Spanish is poor - but it is, slowly, getting better!

COMTAT

● Almudaina

● Cocentaina

Almudaina

On the road from Benimarfull to Planes in the comarca of Comtat is Almudaina, a cherry growing region with just 120 inhabitants. Originally Moorish until they were expelled in the C17[th], there is a unique tower which was originally Roman and then later rebuilt by the moors.

Not quite able to unravel the piece of history concerning this tower. Doña Teresa Gil de Vidaura had lived here and Jaime 1 had wanted her as his wife but later abandoned her when she contracted leprosy. The tower was then also abandoned.

There's a beautiful hotel and spa here, the Hotel Restaurante Els Banys T: 965 530 177 *www.terrola.com*

Tourist Information
T: 965 514 267

Cocentaina

The capital of the Comtat region, Cocentaina has a population of 11,000. While the town has a history linked to both the Moors and the Christians it also features in prehistory. The town sits on the River Serpis. Originally scattered with Moorish farmsteads until the Reconquest, when a Christian quarter was established in the town complete with a wall that was supposed to protect it from the large Moorish population.

A medieval fortified palace can be found in the old Christian quarter. The maze of lanes and alleyways of the old Moorish quarter are interesting to explore.

Cocentaina's centre is considered one of the best preserved medieval centres in the Alicante region. This town is set against the backdrop of the Natural Park of Sierra Mariola.

Cocentaina is get-at-able by bus and train. The town is located next to the N-340 main road. A street market is held on Thursdays and Saturdays.

The nearest city is Alcoy 10kms away, with its hospital, schools and shopping facilities. It is an hour's drive to the coast and 65km from Alicante.

The most easily accessible golf courses are Bonalba and Alicante Golf Club.

Places To Stay
Odón ★ ★ ★ T: 965 591 212, *www.hotelodon.com*

Nou Hostalet, T: 965 592 703, *www.nouhostalet.com*

Batanet, T: 666 852 020, *www.casabatanet.com*

Tourist Information
www.cocentaina.org, T: 965 590 159

70

CASE STUDY
Alberto Kramer from Java, now living in Altea
www.trekearth.com/members/lancehannah/

I was born in Malang, East Java, Indonesia. My mother is Indonesian and my father is Dutch. When I was 14 years old I moved to Holland and a few years later started to travel around as an artist. I came to Spain the first time in the late sixties and loved it. I travelled around and performed in show business for 25 years.

For the last 20 years I have lived in Altea, Alicante where I had a restaurant until last year when I retired. I spend my time travelling and taking photos. I live with my wife, a Spanish woman whom I met in a supermarket.

The best thing for me here is the climate and the ever-changing colours of the sea. The worst is the cost of living here compared with other parts of Spain. It's possible to get value for money in Altea but you have to know where to go!

For someone coming here I would tell them to have patience. Spanish bureaucracy can be really bad. It's a good idea to talk to compatriots living here to get useful information, they probably have gone through the same things you are going through now.

I love Asian food and there are lots of restaurants around for that. There's a vegetable market on Tuesdays in Altea and several big supermarkets. For non-food I do most of my shopping in Alicante (El Corte Inglés). During the summer months there is a handcrafts market in the church square in the evenings.

Altea beach has no sand so I go to Calpe or Benidorm which are close by for my daily walks. My hobby is photography and I move all around this area looking for things to photograph. The weather is great most of the time so I spend a lot of time outside.

MARINA BAJA

Altea

Altea meant "health to all" in its moorish form. It sits on the coast backed by some pretty rugged mountains.

Coincidence or not Altea seems to be a weather line. Every time I have driven through the mountains of Sierra Bernia (1130m) to the north of the town there has been a bank of cloud and even a tad of spitty rain. The once active fishing village is now most popular with tourists thanks to an especially mild micro-climate created by the protective force of these mountains.

It has been described as the cultural capital of Alicante province and is a popular retreat for artists, sculptors and writers. This may explain the pretty new creation, the Miguel Hernandez University of Culture and Fine Arts plus a new concert hall.

Altea's mostly gravel blue flag beaches are Playa de la Olla, Playa del Cap Negret, Playa de la Roda (the city beach), Playa del Cap Blanch and Playa del Mascarat. Playa de Albir just south of the town looks pretty splendid to me as well. Altea also has the Don Cayo 9-hole Golf Club perched on the Sierra Bernia with fabulous views.

Altea's labyrinthine cobbled streets, offering glimpses of the bay, along with its whitewashed house-fronts and palm lined seafront esplanade makes it one of the most beautiful towns in the region. There's a popular street market near the port.

You will easily find the church of *La Mare de Déu del Consol* (Our Lady of Solace) with its blue tiled roof and known for its extraordinary beauty as *"la cupula del mediterraneo"*. Enjoy the view towards Benidorm to the south and Calpe to the north and relish the cool breeze. Pop into *Nuestra Señors de Consuela* then have a long, cold drink or two. In the steep narrow streets leading up to the old town you will find many galleries, arts and crafts and ceramics shops.

Around February 3rd there's the *Mig Any* (Half Year) fiestas celebrating Saint Blaise or San Blas who is believed to intercede in illnesses of the throat. The last week in September is when you will get the almost inevitable Moros y Cristianos Festival, but if it's the fireworks you are after then the fiesta celebrating the Feast of San Lorenzo 12-14 August is the big one here. The display is over the sea and is rumoured to be the best one in Spain.

Cactusland North of Altea on the N-332, a private botanical garden specialising in cacti.

Places To Stay
Meliá Altea Hills Resort ★★★★★ T: 966 881 006

Meliá Villa Gadea Thalasso – Spa ★★★★★ T: 966 817 100

Altaya ★★ T: 965 840 800, *www.hotelaltaya.com*

Ábaco Inn, T: 966 882 500, *www.abacoinnaltea.com*

Tourist Information
www.altea.es, T: 965 841 300

Downtown Altea   © Alberto Kramer

L'Alfàs del Pi

L'Alfàs del Pi is in the comarca of Marina Baja and forms a triangle with Altea and Benidorm, which encompasses the interesting area of the Sierra Helada. Close by is the town and Playa de Albir.

L'Alfàs del Pi is a small town with a fortress that was built for protection against Berber pirate attacks. The name Alfàs del Pi, *sown land*, appropriately describes the area, characterized by residential zones, with an active cultural activity. In July, the town is illuminated for the celebration of its famous film festival.

Places To Stay
Albir Playa Hotel ★★★★ T: 966 864 943, *www.albirplayahotel.com*

Kaktus Albir ★★★★ T: 966 864 830, *www.kaktusgrup.com*

Rober Palas ★★★ T: 966 864 312, *www.roberpalas.com*

El Ventorrillo, T: 966 866 186

La Riviera, T: 966 865 386, *www.hotellariviera.es*

Noguera, T: 966 866 153

Albir Garden, T: 966 805 916

Tourist Information
www.lalfas.com, T: 965 888 905

Benidorm

Its modest population of roughly 70,000 inhabitants swells to well over half a million during the summer as tourists (especially British) flock to soak up the sea, sand, sun and family friendly atmosphere.

Before the tourist industry in Spain began in earnest in the 60s Benidorm was a small village. Today it is a thriving, bustling town with sprawling, high-rise hotels and apartment blocks. However I remember a number of my elderly relatives who came to Benidorm for the winter months as it was possible for them to live better and cheaper than staying in the UK.

Benidorm's three major beaches: Levante, Poniente and Mal Pas all have blue flag status. Actually as I write Poniente has had its flag withdrawn because of the development of a paseo but I am sure this is temporary.

Despite the massive building developments it still retains a green, spacious, ambience thanks to Pedro Zaragoza Ortis, who in 1954 created the Plan General de Ordenación that ensured every building would have an area of 'leisure' land, guaranteeing a future free of cramped concrete construction which are the blight of other resorts in Spain.

Pedro Zaragoza Ortis

Pedro Zaragoza Ortis, who died aged 85, is credited with turning Benidorm into a destination for mass-tourism. When Zaragoza - a former phosphate miner and railway porter - took over as mayor of Benidorm in 1950 it was a sleepy Spanish fishing village with few amenities.

There are English pubs and bars serving fish and chips, fry-ups, warm beer and other delicacies demanded by the British sun-seeker on the Costa Blanca. While there is now a resident population of some 70,000, in the summer this number reaches half a million; many of these visitors returning year after year.

This transformation was largely the work of Zaragoza, the mayor for 17 years. He visualised a small town with pretty plazas and boulevards, lush gardens and comfortable hotels. He arranged for water to be pumped to Benidorm from 10 miles away, then set about encouraging package tour operators to fly planeloads of tourists to Spain.

It was primarily the British who responded, and the women brought with them the bikini, leading to the most famous episode in Zaragoza's career as mayor. He had seen the two-piece swimming costumes in magazines, and knew that in northern Europe they were considered unremarkable. In Spain, however, they were banned by General Franco's regime.

In 1953 on the principle that "you couldn't stop it" Zaragoza authorised the wearing of bikinis at Benidorm. No one in the country had attempted this, and there was uproar. As members of the Civil Guard scuffled with scantily-clad girls on Benidorm's beaches, the local archbishop threatened to excommunicate Zaragoza, who decided to appeal directly to Franco. At 6am one morning he set off for Madrid on his Vespa motor scooter, arriving in the Spanish capital eight hours later. "I changed my shirt but I went in to the General with my trousers spattered with motor oil," he later claimed. "He backed me, and the bikini stayed."

As Benidorm was gradually transformed, he became an enthusiast for high-rise architecture, taking the view that by building upwards, more people could be by the sea and he could still maintain green areas around each apartment block.

There are 330 skyscrapers in Benidorm: in Europe only London, Frankfurt and Moscow have more. The town also boasts the tallest building in Spain - the 4-star 'Gran Hotel Bali' towering at 186 metres. Each summer the city plays host to the Benidorm International Song Festival.

Today 10 million holidaymakers visit Benidorm every year, making it Europe's third busiest destination after London and Paris. Although the British remain the principal market, it is also popular with Dutch and Belgian tourists and plenty of Spaniards. It has a reputation, among Spanish pensioners, for being the best place in Spain for picking up partners.

Favel, my mother-in-law, knows Benidorm well.

Favel on Benidorm

It is a town you either love or hate. I personally like it. It's a fairly large town divided into two sections by the old town which is very pleasant with lots of winding streets and shops, restaurants and bars – very pretty in places.

On one side is the Poniente beach and district and on the other is Levante beach and district. They are very good large beaches and lots of entertainment going on most of the time. At night-time the Benidorm Palace is well worth a visit. It's quite an experience and good value for money. You get a very good three-course meal and as much wine as you can drink (while you are eating wine is included in the cost). You can dance and dance and then there is a fabulous live show always; it is said the stage is the largest in Europe.

My friends and neighbours often used to make up a party and take a coach up from Ciudad Quesada. Never got home much before the wee small hours and most of us were over 60!

I always enjoy a visit to Benidorm at any time of the year.

There is certainly no shortage of accommodation, restaurants, shops and nightlife. The town may be disconcerting for those looking for a quiet place to stay, but for energetic types who can loll on the beach all day and party all night, this is the place to be. Its fine, sandy, clean beaches and transparent water are what have made Benidorm the tourist centre that it is today.

The most popular beach is the **Playa de Levante**, 2km from the old town centre and in the height of summer, there may be little room to manoeuvre.

Benidorm skyline and Playa de Levante

The slightly quieter **Playa de Poniente** is situated on the edge of the old town centre. The white stone balcony at the historical centre of the town, Canfali vantage point, affords generous views over the town. There's a huge range of leisure activities for all ages of tourists, from water sports in the day and hardcore nightlife, to peaceful walks through the park and excursions to the Sierra Gelada (or Sierra Helada) nearby.

The Sierra Gelada (Frozen Mountain) is a large parque natural of something approaching 6000 hectares. It appears to have been losing many of its important plants and the gardeners are busily rectifying this by replacing endangered species "cultivated from seeds taken from the Sierra Helada in years gone by".

In an article of "Walking on Spain's Costa Blanca" by Alpine Exploratory, *www.alpineexploratory.com*, an organisation that helps inveterate walkers and hikers to have great self-guided holidays and is into responsible tourism (*Take only photos, leave only footprints...*) I found this description:

> " - *a 6km long wedge of land rising up from the plain to a summit at 435m (1,427ft) and ending abruptly at cliffs dropping straight down to the Mediterranean Sea. Streets, then lanes and then paths lead from the East end of Benidorm to a high lookout point that marks the start of the Sierra Helada ridge and its many undulations on the way to the summit - a great walk.*"

A large fruit and vegetable market is held on Tuesdays, the street market on Wednesdays and on Sundays there's a busy flea market. There is also a synagogue which services the Jewish community of the province. Don Cayo Golf Club is 13km north of Benidorm.

Benidorm sits on the A-7 autovia just above Alicante and therefore very accessible to visitors.

Benidorm's theme parks include Terra Mítica, Terra Natura, Aqualandia and Mundomar which are located just outside the city. There is also the tiny Isla de Benidorm if you fancy a boat trip.

Places To Stay
Gran Hotel Villaitana Wellness Golf & Business Sun ★★★★★
T: 966 803 852

Castilla ★★★★ T: 965 851 514

Gran Hotel Bali ★★★★ T: 966 815 200,
www.granhotelbali.com

Madeira Centro ★★★★ T: 965 854 950,
www.madeiracentro.com

Les Dunes Comodoro ★★★ T: 966 802 126, *www.lesdunes.es*

Poseidón ★★★ T: 965 850 200, *www.hotelesposeidon.com*

Rosamar ★★★ T: 965 850 502, *www.hotelrosamar.com*

Rocamar ★ T: 965 850 552

Milord's Suites, T: 966 831 600, *www.milords.es*

Lope de Vega, T: 965 854 154

Tourist Information
www.benidorm.org, T: 965 855 500

Cala de Finestrat

Known as La Cala, this once little town and its small bay is just to the west of Benidorm. It is actually divided between the towns of Finestrat and Villajoyosa. Most people would now consider it as part of Benidorm because the more famous town has grown right down to the borders of Cala Finestrat.

In fact, one of Benidorm's greatest symbols, the Hotel Gran Bali, is actually in the Cala de Finestrat. It's a great place for tapas and other more international foods.

La Cala sits very close to many of the family theme parks.

Callosa d'Ensarriá

The *Fuentes de Algar*, natural swimming pools and water cascades, are three kilometers from here and everybody I know who has ever been there describe this place in glowing and positive terms.

Finestrat

Sitting below the second highest mountain of the region Puig Campana at 1,408m, Finestrat has a population of 1500 and is a more tranquil place than the surrounding towns. Its one and two storey houses are perched on top of rocky outcrops and backed by dramatic mountain scenery. The traditional aspects of the village have not been drowned out by massive urbanisations and tourism here is more low-key.

The *Ermito de la Remedio* is constructed on a vantage point giving excellent views of the whole of the Marina Baja.

A street market is held on Fridays. The town is less than 15 minutes drive from Benidorm and Villajoyosa and on the road to Sella.

Places To Stay
Alone ★ ★ ★ T: 965 855 750, *www.medsur-hoteles.com*

Tropic ★ ★ ★ T: 966 812 128, *www.hoteltropic.com*

Cala ★ ★ T: 965 854 662, *www.hotel-lacala.com*

La Plantación, T: 965 788 715, *www.laplantacion.com*

Tourist Information
www.finestrat.org, T: 965 878 100

Guadalest

Guadalest is very much on the tourist map despite or because of it being a tiny village of about 200 people and perched on a pinnacle. The village is entered through a tunnel carved through the rock.

Originally Moorish it was conquered by Jaime 1 and ceded to Sarria and later to Aragon. There are innumerable museums and lots of souvenir shops, restaurants and so on.

The views are magnificent. If you consider the wider area this is real climbing country, particularly from Abdet. I am not a climbing person myself – I can barely climb out of bed – but there seem to be some seriously good crags in this area. For more information see *www.freewebs.com/costablancarock* for a directory of the crags.

Just a little beyond Guadelest is El Arca at Benmantell which is a Wild Animal Refuge supported by Reina Sophia.

And in the valley below is an (artificial) emerald green lake which makes for yet another outstanding memory of this area.

Places To Stay
Destino Guadalest, T: 966 112 064, *www.destinoguadalest.com*

Cases Noves, T: 676 010 171

Tourist Information
www.guadalest.es, T: 965 885 095

La Nucia

This is largely a residential zone, with 69 housing estates occupied by a number of foreign residents. The village has retained its original charm with white houses looking down over the slopes of the mountains out onto the coast. There is a rastro market held on Sunday mornings, where second-hand goods stalls stretch for over 2km through the village. The street market is on Mondays and Fridays.

La Nucia is easily accessible, located on the main road 5km from the A-7 motorway and 10km from Benidorm.

Don Cayo Golf Club is less than 10 minutes drive away.

Places To Stay
Apartamentos Casa Carmen, T: 965 873 492

Casa Rural Castañeto, T: 965 153 195

Casa Bonita Marina Baixa, T: 965 873 871

Tourist Information
www.lanucia.es, *T:* 966 895 672

Polop

This is another of the small (just over 3500 inhabitants) medieval towns worth a leisurely walk through. There is a Sunday rastro at the polígono industrial.

Polop also has a museum **Pequeña Costa Mágica** which just might appeal to young and old. It is a collection of crafted buildings and artefacts put together literally by Antonio Marco Martinez. As this area is also the centre of tin plate toy industry it should come as no surprise that someone has created something special. See *www.pequenocastamagica.com* T: 966 896 773 for details.

Places To Stay
Casa Ivars, T: 965 870 051

Casa Maquila, T: 965 842 936, *www.casaruralmaquila.com*

La Casa Blanca, T: 626 244 527

Tourist Information
www.polop.org, T: 966 896 072

Relleu

This is an alternative route up or down to Sella and beyond. Another little village with a ravaged Moorish castillo it sits within the beautiful sierra del Aguilar with commanding views over the coast.

Places To Stay
Casa Rural Genoveva I, T: 965 863 634

L'Aguilar, T: 965 863 634

Sella

A small village in the Aitana mountains on the road from Villajoyosa (18kms) and Finestrat. The area is heavily tiered for almonds and lemons. There is a real charm about the area.

For some authentic Spanish food and atmosphere try Bar "Fonda" situated in the centre of the village which is quite well known although it is some years since I have dined there. The bar has tea towels hanging on the walls from all over the world. It was always somewhere you had to book particularly for Sunday lunch. A recent visit to the area shows some road improvement and more tiering on the hillside but more for housing than the usual almond and lemon crops.

My mother-in-law Favel has been there many times.

Favel on Sella

Sella is a small village up on the mountains behind Benidorm, inland of course; a pretty little village with a church way up on the hill. There is a cafe bar when approaching the village of Sella called "Fonda", which is very popular for its food and ambience. Everything is home made including cold meats, sausages, tortilla, and wine. You can buy bottles of wine to take away if you wish and at very reasonable prices. Very Spanish. Don't go there if you are in a hurry though as the meal is likely to take quite a time but be well worth it. The last two times I have been there I arrived at 1.30pm and left at 6pm – once we got caught up with a big Spanish party that was going on there at the time. Great fun.

Not far beyond Sella is the Guhyaloka Buddist Retreat Centre near Font del Arc (*www.guhyaloka.com*). This means "secret realm" which is probably highly descriptive and the centre has all kinds of retreats for men only. Apart from anything else they have a masterpiece of perfect instructions on how to get there from Alicante airport without a car.

Places To Stay
Casa Rural El Mirador, T: 965 879 000

Finca Seguró, T: 965 972 575

La Palmera, T: 965 972 258

Villa Picó, T: 965 879 238, *www.villapico.com*

Tourist Information
T: 965 879 001

Tárbena

Tárbena is located between mountains, this lovely village is in the north of Marina Baja and is a peaceful place with a population of 800, set in terraced agricultural land. Its white houses with their ochre tiled roofs are gathered around an old village church. Its mountainside position means that the village has views that take in Benidorm and its coastline. There is a teepee colony outside the village inhabited by people seeking an alternative, rural lifestyle.

Tárbena has eight bars run by various nationalities including English.

Places To Stay
De Tárbena ★★ T: 965 884 006, *www.hotel-tarbena.com*

Casa Rural Carmen, T: 965 884 056

Casa Teresita, T: 965 884 038

Es Bon Pastor, T: 965 884 007

Tourist Information
T: 965 884 234

Villajoyosa

Villajoyosa (or La Vila Joiosa in Catalan) is a seaside fishing town just south of Benidorm. It is divided by a river estuary. As the historical capital of Marina Baja, Villajoyosa is a slightly quieter alternative to Benidorm. Painted in a multitude of colours, deep blue, banana yellow and apple green, the original purpose of these painted facades was to ensure that sailors could see their homes from far out at sea.

Villajoyosa has 4km of beaches, the most popular of which is the Centro beach.

Villajoyosa (La Vila for short) means Joyful Village, which is a fitting name for a town famous for its chocolate and brightly coloured houses.

Driving through Villajoyosa used to be hell. Nowadays it is much improved by a new road behind the main part of town. The coastal train service from the town enables you to get as far as Dénia in the north and Alicante to the south stopping frequently to take in pretty coastal villages and resorts such as nearby Benidorm. Car parking underground on the front makes good sense. The puerto end of town (to the east) looks a pretty good bet for leisurely eating if you aren't intending to swim.

The Valor chocolate factory (*www.valor.es*) offers free tours (good business tactic!) and Villajoyosa's Gothic Catholic church and bridges dating back to Roman times provide plenty to see. If you're into shopping then check out the weekly market each Thursday morning and there is a daily afternoon fish auction.

The nearest golf club is that of Don Cayo, 13km north of Benidorm.

A typical Villajoyosa street

As well as the Royal Palm Casino, the town's new amphitheatre hosts various performances throughout the year and it's worth checking its programme.

Villajoyosa's world-famous Moors and Christians battles are re-enacted in the last week of July each year. Although similar fiestas and re-enactments can be found in other Spanish towns this is the place to experience it at its best. Normally the town's beaches would be blue flagged but this status was lost in 2008 probably due to building works on the paseo.

Places To Stay
El Montíboli ★ ★ ★ ★ ★ T: 965 890 250

Euro Tennis, T: 965 891 250, *www.hoteleurotennis.com*

Tourist Information
www.villajoyosa.com, T: 966 851 001

CASE STUDY
Garry Holland from Liverpool, living in Formentera del Segura
www.eels-sp.com

I was initially born in Liverpool, but moved over here from Bournemouth, and I now live in Formentera del Segura with my wife and my dog.

In England I had an English academy and taught English as a second language, over here I kept some of my contracts and teach business English to non-native speakers.

The best thing is the peace and tranquillity, being close enough to all of the amenities and far enough away not to be bothered by them. The worst thing is the English people who think that they are better than everyone else and think everything should be like it is in England. Not all Brits are like that of course but some of them are.

The best advice is research everything very carefully and get an insurance cover against anything that can go wrong when purchasing a property so that you can get your money back.

The airport is half an hour away as is Elche, Murcia and Alicante. The beach is 10 minutes drive and we have a lot of markets during the week in the different villages/towns within 15 minutes drive.

There are many different types of restaurants, plenty of English bars as well as Spanish. The main problem here is that you do not get chance to practice your Spanish unless you go out of the area or join a Spanish club, and the British reputation is not the best in the world.

ALCOIÀ

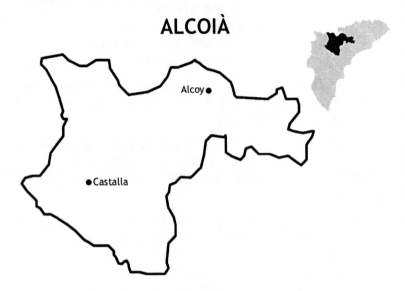

Alcoy

Alcoy (Alcoi in Valencian) sits on the N-340 south of Cocentaina. I remember a series of bends on this road in the Sierra de Penarroja as you go in the direction of Jijona. Spectacular countryside, but keep your eyes on the road if you are driving. The local industry is mainly paper and textile, with very little agriculture not surprisingly as it is very hilly.

The old city was a surprise and had an ambience of sophistication, which impressed me. The town is big (62,000 inhabitants) enough to have lanes for buses and taxis alone. The Placa de Dins or Plaza Major just has to be the place to stop for a while and enjoy a coffee or a cerveza to absorb the essence of the place.

Definitely a place to dump the car for a while and raise your eyes and follow your nose around the historic areas. Possibly indulge in a little shopping? Passing through just doesn't cut it.

Directly quoted from a plaque in the square:

> *"This main square called Placa de Dins preserves the Classicist arches of the cloister of the Monastery of Saint Augustine. It was built in the 14th century and subsequently refurbished in 1837 after the assets of the Church and religious communities were seized. The Monastery was acquired by the Town Hall and fitted out as housing and market. The architect who made the refurbishment and the extension was Jose Molto Valor. A Gothic arch survives in one of the access to this square from Saint Tomas Street. This is the only vestige of Saint Augustine's Church that once rose by the Monastery."*

Alcoy is very mountainous and covered with Mediterranean pines. The Parque Natural del Font Roja is south west of the town and the Sierra de Marriola (with a peak of 1390m) makes its presence felt close by.

The main fiesta is the Moors and Christians mock battles held in April (22nd-24th) for the Battle of Alcoy (1275) when St George helped defeat the Moorish forces lead by Al Azraq. Alcoyans believe this is the best fiesta in Spain (probably the world!) and they prepare all year round for this 4-day orgy of fun, food and fighting. The year begins and ends in April for those people in one of the 28 Moorish or Christian armies!

The idiom "tener más moral que el Alcoyano" (to have greater morale than an Alcoyano) is used across Spain to describe an untiringly persistent person. The story goes that local football team (CD Alcoyano) were many goals down in a football match but every time the referee was about to blow the final whistle the Alcoyano players would plead for more time so they could bring the score back to a draw.

Places To Stay
AC Ciutat d'Alcoi ★★★★ T: 965 333 606

Reconquista ★★★ T: 965 330 900

Savoy ★ T: 965 547 272, *www.hostalsavoy.com*

Casa Rural El Pinet, T: 609 617 280

El Teularet, T: 966 523 173

Tourist Information
www.alcoiturisme.com, T: 965 537 100

Castalla

Dominated by a castle, Castalla is part of an area which experienced much fighting and warring back as far as Neolithic times and later between Muslims and Christians, pushed around by the two Pedros and ending up with Aragon. In the War of the Spanish Succession Castalla sided with the Bourbons. It was also the site for two major battles during the War of Independence. The Spanish lost heavily in the first in 1812 but led by General Suchet the Spanish then routed the French in 1813. King Ferdinand Vll created the Cross of Distinction inscribed Castalla April 13, 1813. Castalla was awarded City status in 1889.

The village has a well-preserved old centre with steep narrow streets that lead up to the hermitage and castle. Forest covers 51% of the area around here and is a great base for walking.

Places To Stay
Xorret del Cati ★★★ T: 965 560 400, *www.ghihoteles.com*

Don José ★★ T: 965 561 505

Tourist Information
www.castalla.org, T: 966 560 801

ALTO VINALOPÓ

Biar

With fewer than 4000 inhabitants, Biar is an ancient town with a 12th century walled Moorish castle which became a national monument in 1931. It had been a Roman town prior to this and was known then as Apiarum – referring to its special relationship with bees!

The *Moros y Cristianos* festival of Biar is celebrated each year from May 10th to 13th.

Places To Stay
Finca Les Fanecaes ★ T: 902 220 052

Mas Fontanelles ★ T: 686 426 126, *www.masfontanelles.com*

La Façana, T: 965 810 373, *www.lafasana.com*

Ca Tona III, T: 963 846 775

Tourist Information
www.turismo.biar.es, T: 965 811 177

Cañada
Close to Villena is the village of Cañada with a population of 1500. Its white houses are clustered around a hill, the top of which is a sanctuary to the Virgin del Carmen, the patron saint of sailors. A fiesta in her honour takes place in July. The Mystery Play is also celebrated enthusiastically in Cañada.

"Little Break"   © Alberto Kramer

Sax

Also known as Cabreras, Sax is one of the historical and cultural towns in Alto Vinalopo. The Moorish castillo of Sax stands proud above the town, spectacular under floodlights at night, it was conquered by the Castilians in 1239.

There are some important climbs in this area, Penas del Rey is the most major ascent. Behind the town is a nature reserve Sierra de Salinas with a small salt lake. There is a snow cave and a good Archaeology Museum. Moors and Christians celebrations are between 1st and 14th February.

Places To Stay
Fuente El Cura, T: 966 969 013

Tourist Information
www.sax.es, T: 965 474 006

Villena

The capital of L'Alt Vinalopó with a population of 33,000 is Villena. It is an important communications centre, serving as a crossroads between Castile, Murcia and Valencia. Due to its position, the city has a rich history and continues to thrive today.

There are several historic buildings of interest to be found amongst the architecture of modern day Villena. The town is spread around an ancient Moorish castle, L'Atalaya, an imposing building with battlements and a double enclosure wall that has witnessed many historic battles.

A combination of Gothic and Renaissance architecture can be found at the church of Santa María, with its tall vaulted domes supported by graceful twisted columns.

The Chapí Theatre, named after the musical genius Ruperto Chapí who was a native of Villena, is a quirky building. It was built in the early twentieth century over a number of years in a variety of architectural styles, the result being an art deco kind of flavour.

An interesting Festival Museum is located in Santiago Square, displaying collections of old costumes and posters from the traditional Moors and Christians Festival that is played out annually in towns and villages across the entire region.

Villena is associated with the great Spanish tennis player, Juan Carlos Ferrera through a tennis academy founded here in 1995 by Antonio Martinez Cascales to continue the exceptional training of young Spanish under-14 players of which Ferrera is a classic example. For more detail see: *www.equelite.com*

You will find all the amenities you would expect from a large and modern town, with a national railway and good road connections. A weekly market takes place on Thursdays. It is 59km to Alicante Airport on the N-330 Motorway.

The old Bullring in Villena

The nearest golf course is Alenda Golf Club, 40km away and paragliding is popular in the Sierra de la Villa nearby.

Places To Stay
Salvadora ★ T: 965 800 950

Casa el Procurador, T: 965 979 161

Tourist Information
www.untesoro.villena.es, T: 966 150 236

CASE STUDY
Richard & Nicola from the Midlands with a finca in Sax
The Inland Magazine *www.timspain.com*

We are originally from Solihull in the West Midlands where we ran a business for 11 years. We now live in the campo outside of Sax, my wife and myself and our two young children as well as a variety of pets and other animals.

We run a magazine called The Inland Magazine, which is not only distributed to many inland towns/villages, but also to 14 coastal towns.

The best things about where we live, are the views, the privacy if you require it, the tranquillity the friendliness of the Spanish of which we have many friends and also the easiness of gaining access to almost anywhere in Spain, as the road links here are phenomenal. There is not one single drawback of where we live, it is next to perfect for all that we require.

Our home is sited on the Camara mountain overlooking the village of Sax, the plot that it sits on is 8,700 sq mtrs in size, we have two properties on this plot one is a four bed finca and the other is a two bed, two bath, kitchen dinner which is sited 100 yds away from the main house. The second house is used for family and friends when they come over to visit. We also have a large pool in the middle of the two houses and a Jacuzzi for 7 people. The views from our home are breathtaking, with a direct

---

view of Sax and its castle and mountains all around, the wildlife is also something to behold.

If you are thinking of moving to inland Spain, remember that you will be living amongst Spanish, so you will need to integrate and be willing to learn at least some of their language. Also if you require privacy then the coast is definitely not somewhere that you would like to live.

The food in the area is the basic Valencian diet, but there are also three very good restaurants within a ten minute drive whom serve varying menus from around the world. There is a market in the main town every week where you can purchase fresh fruit and veg at prices that are really incomparable in most other countries. The next town along, Petrer-Elda has four markets per week.

As for the beaches, we do not tend to pay to much attention to visiting these as they are very crowded in the peak months. On the very odd occasion if we go to the beach, it is the beach at El Altet just past the airport, this takes around 30 minutes to get to. Every Summer evening the whole family goes walking around the roads and tracks that wind along the mountain side where you can spot numerous wildlife eg eagles, owls, snakes, foxes - the list is endless.

VINALOPÓ MEDIO

Petrel
Elda
Monóvar
Pinoso
Novelda
Monforte del Cid
Aspe

Aspe

Aspe is a large town of over 18,000, just off the A-7 and is fairly rural still. There has been a great deal of road building locally and it probably needs some time to recover.

You can tell you're entering Aspe from any direction by the characteristic bagged grapes in the vineyards. These grapes make their way to tables all around Spain on New Year's Eve.

Some attempt is being made to create nature walks in the area. Jose Galvan a painter who was well known in Paris lived here.
Thereis also a Moorish castle.

Places To Stay

Ya, T: 965 495 051

Mayordomo, T: 965 492 661

Holihouse Viviendas Vacacionales, T: 965 492 704

Tourist Information

www.ayto-villadeaspe.es, T: 966 919 900

Elda

If you have a shoe fetish then Elda is the place for you. Elda and the adjacent town of Petrer are separated by just one street, together they form the largest urban area of El Vinalopó Mitja with a combined population of 81,000.

Like the neighbouring city of Elche, the manufacture of shoes is the industrial focus and the town's shoe museum displays an interesting array of footwear from around the globe.

The town is of Moorish origin and contains the Church of Santa Ana, which was originally built as a mosque. The semi-ruined Elda castle is on a hill to the north of the city. Although Petrer is just 4km away from Elda's centre, its inhabitants speak Valenciano whereas the people of Elda speak Spanish.

Elda has plenty of schools, including a university, a new hospital, a 10-screen cinema complex and a Carrefour hypermarket and shopping centre complete with drive-through McDonalds.

There is also a huge indoor market selling fresh produce open 6 days a week. An open-air market is held on Tuesdays and Saturdays, selling clothes, shoes and other goods.

Elda has a national RENFE railway station with fast connections to Alicante, Murcia and the rest of Spain. Elda is easily accessible from Alicante which is 36km away via the N-330 motorway. It is about 30 minutes drive to the coast. Alenda Golf Club is 18km away.

Places To Stay

AC Elda ★★★★ T: 966 981 221

Elda, T: 965 380 556

Santa Ana, T: 965 380 231

Tourist Information

www.elda.es, T: 965 380 402

Monforte del Cid

The village is typically Moorish in appearance with a labyrinth of streets around an ancient mosque, which is now a church. An agricultural town, grapes are amongst its produce.

There are also distilleries producing spirits. Try an aniseed drink called *paloma monfortina* a 14th century invention. Good luck!

There's a market on Wednesdays and Fridays.

Tourist Information

www.monfortedelcid.es, T: 965 620 025

Monóvar

Monóvar is within Vinalopo Media with a population of about 12,000. It is a very Spanish town, in many ways very self-contained and even has its own Arts Theatre. It sits at the eastern end of a series of valleys stretching from Jumilla where the major crop is vines for winemaking.

Monóvar has its own interesting bodega El Primitivo. Interestingly the owner refused to put his wine through the D.O. The desert wine *El Fondillón* comes from Monóvar.

As well as wine Monóvar produces footwear and leather. Alicante's red marble is extracted from the quarries around the town.

Tourist Information
www.monover.com, T: 966 960 311

Novelda

Novelda sits close to the northern route out of Alicante. Very much in the area where marble is mined. Well worth a visit if you like Gaudí architecture as there is a modernist Gaudí-like church Santuario de Santa Maria made of local marble and stone. Novelda has other modernist gems to see particularly the Casa-Museo Modernista, a house designed by Pedro Cerdan.

Wednesday is market day.

Places To Stay
Pasaje, T: 965601250

Suiza, T: 965601996

Tourist Information
www.novelda.es, T: 965 609 228

Petrer

Petrer abuts Elda to the point that it is now generally listed as the conurbation of Elda-Petrer. Castillo Petrer is of Muslim origin from 12th century. Its true beginnings lie within the Muslim village of Bitran although there is a lot of evidence around of Neolithic and Celtic Iberian settlement. A great day out for those interested in medieval history and castle towns would be a tour of Petrer, Castalla, Onil, Biar & Jijona.

The town has its own Moros y Cristianos celebrations in mid-May and honours Saint Boniface the martyr. You can see some of the recent fiesta on the following site - *www.petrerenfestes.com*

Tourist Information
www.petrer.es, T: 966 376 968

Pinoso

Pinoso is a very Spanish town reliant on marble and wine growing. Their fiesta patronal is from the 1st to the 10th of August, with young bulls roaming the streets.

They do wine well! I had an interesting red wine, loads of ice and I think soda at 11am in the undercover market on a very warm day. It was delicious. Also they produce good meats and artisan products. There are a couple of pretty sierras heading up toward Yecla and Jumilla (in Murcia) which are worth a drive.

Places To Stay
Monte Carmelo, T: 965 477 126

El Sequé, T: 965 478 702

Tourist Information
www.pinosoturismo.es, T: 902 190 900

ALCANTÍ

Aigües

The name means "water" in Valencian. There is a thermal spa in the district which contains minerals with medicinal qualities where children with tuberculosis used to be treated. At the present time it is a small village with a population of around 800.

However Aigües is about to have a major new tourist development - the Balneario de Aigües. It has apparently recently been bought by the owner of a local football team and is to be resurrected with a very large injection of cash.

The Balneario

The Balneario de Aigües retained its splendour until the 1930s and then in 1936 it was bought by the State and was destined to become 'El Preventorio' a sanitarium for childhood tuberculosis. After the civil war and due to the disappearance of the sickness, the building lost its raison d'etre and fell into disrepair with passing of time.

On the first Sunday of each month during the summer there's an artisan market with paintings, sculptures and local produce.

Places To Stay

Finca el Otero, T: 965 690 116, *www.fincaelotero.com*

Entre Medianeras, T: 965 143 113

Tourist Information

www.aigues.es, T: 965 690 061

Alicante (Alacant)

Alicante city is the capital of the Alicante province, and the heart of the region of Alicante. This thriving cosmopolitan city has three thousand years of history behind it but has entered the 21st century as a leading centre of commerce, culture and tourism.

The port of Alicante straddles the coast with the magnificent backdrop of the Benacantil Mountains. Alicante has a very mild climate with winter temperatures averaging 16-17°C. It boasts a wealth of beaches including an open beach of 7 kilometres, a secluded beach protected by a headland, an urban beach that is located next to the port and one south of the city in Agua Amarga.

Alicante's impressive seafront promenade is the palm-fringed Paseo de la Explanada, lined with street cafes and inlaid with red, cream and black marble. The night life is concentrated around the old city centre known as El Barrio.

A city of 332,000 this historic Mediterranean port is one of Spain's fastest growing cities thanks to the huge influx of tourists visiting the Costa Blanca beaches every year with Alicante airport at El Altet serving many international and budget airlines and located a mere 11km south of the city. At the time of writing (2008) the airport has opened a second terminal particularly serviced by Easyjet. There are a zillion car rental companies located here too, see the airports section for details.

A boat in the bay approaching Castillo de Santa Barbara

Alicante has a newish (2003) tramline connecting the harbour to the suburb of El Campello making it easy for tourists and locals in the city to get to the beach. Further tram connections into Benidorm are currently in progress.

There is a spacious harbour which hosts regular ferry services to the Balearic Islands.

Above the city, Castillo de Santa Barbara offers an amazing view of the town and harbour. Like a fairytale castle high on a hill, the Castillo de Santa Barbara rests on the summit of Mount Benacantil with the city and the Med spread out below. With drawbridge, secret passages and dungeon it dates back to medieval times, and exploring the castle can provide hours of fun.

> *The Castillo can be accessed by a lift from Playa del Postiguet.*

Playa del Postiguet - is located at the foot of the Santa Barbara Castle. This beach has bean awarded a Blue Flag and has lifeguards, a watchtower, a Red Cross post, and, amongst other facilities access for the handicapped. The beach is sandy and popular with tourists and has the usual fare of Irish pubs (mostly run by Spaniards) serving draught beer. In the summer mini "hippy colonies" are known to spring up with people making their accommodation on the beach.

Museo de la Asegurada – Once a formidable prison and munitions store, today this 17th century building is a museum and reflects *mans' higher consciousness* with collections of art by Gris, Miro, Picasso and Dali, and the lesser-known works of Spanish painters such as Chillida, Mompo and Zobel.

The Marq Museum is a must for anyone interested in the history and prehistory of the area. For more information see *www.marqalicante.com* or T: 965 149 006.

At the foot of the main entrance to the Ayuntamiento (town hall) is the "cota cero" (zero point) which is used as a reference to measure the height above or below sea level of any point in Spain.

Alicante's main fiesta, the Bonfires of Saint Juan, takes place at the time of the summer solstice.

San Juan with its fine golden sand and 8km beach has many facilities, including showers, volleyball nets, beach bars (chiringitos), pedal boat hire, parking, children's playground, etc. There are dozens of restaurants lined all along the promenade, allowing beach goers to not only spend the day on San Juan Beach, but also to enjoy some gastronomy on the Costa Blanca.

Alicante is great for buying ceramics, woodcarvings, and hand-tooled leather items, with outlets on just about every street corner. Modern sculptures in wood, marble and stone can be bought at the studio of Pedro Soriano at the Plaza San Antonio 2.

Daily markets are held at Paseo Gadia which are especially good for jewellery, leather goods and cheap watches. The market comes to life in the evening. On Thursdays and Saturdays, there's a street market selling goods ranging from fruit and vegetables to clothes.

As a Nativespainer who is still hooked on the John Lewis partnership I am happy to say that Alicante has a branch of El Corte Inglés for the more mundane, every day necessities of life like Liz Claiborne trousers which actually fit this rather pearshaped English body.

Nearby Cala del Pichon close to the Royal Sports Club offers a little sandy cove, an ideal spot for a bit of fishing off its breakwater.

There are 4 golf courses within easy reach of Alicante.

At Playa de San-Juan-Condomina you will find Alicante Golf Club *www.alicantegolf.com* and El Plantio Golf Club *www.elplantio.com* is nearby. The other two are Alendi *www.alendagolf.com* and at Bonalba *www.golfbonalba.com*.

One of the best places to visit at night is the old city centre known as El Barrio. Here you'll find a host of bars, taverns, cervecerias (beer cellars) and pizza joints. Each has its own style and personality and you'll nearly always find live music - from salsa and jazz to rock and flamenco.

The modern zone, between Alfonso El Sabio and the Explanada, offers other types of entertainment, with elegant pubs, sophisticated restaurants with famed cuisine, clubs and dance halls. In the summer months you'll also find plenty of music, dancing and entertainment down at the beach of San Juan.

An unusual and highly successful initiative by the local government has seen the introduction of a special night train called the "Trensnochador". This service, established in 1988, runs from 9pm to 7am stopping at the neighbouring towns along the coast to enable holidaymakers to enjoy the wealth of nightlife on offer outside the city boundaries.

It's an excellent project which enables local residents and tourists alike to travel to and from nightspots with ease and safety. Around 70% of its passengers are aged between 16 and 21 and 60% of those are female. The train is well lit, provides on board entertainment and a ticket includes discounts for local bars, clubs and discos. It helps to reduce drink driving and its users avoid the parking headaches which plague Alicante and other major resorts such as Benidorm. The train starts in the city and stops at Playa San Juan, El Campello, Villajoyosa, Benidorm and Altea.

Alicante has a full calendar of fiestas throughout the year, providing some colourful and raucous night-time entertainment in true Spanish style. The biggest and arguably the best is Les Fogueres de Sant Joan when dozens of giant wooden and papier-mâché effigies are erected at all the city's major street inter-sections. The effigies are beautifully sculptured and painted tableaux taking a satirical look at some of the major issues of the day. You may not understand the issues but you won't fail to be impressed when the locals set fire to them all and the city becomes a giant bonfire! Just a word of warning here as the fiestas also include daily bull fights, which are not my cup of tea and maybe not of others.

The big night is June 24th with the burning of the effigies followed by a spectacular firework display. But the fiesta continues until June 29th, overlapping with another celebration, the Feast of San Pedro which sees a riot of colourful processions, bands and more fireworks. Pop along to one of the "barracas" - the makeshift fiesta houses which provide the focus for outdoor music, dancing and revelling until the small hours.

Places To Stay

Sidi San Juan ★★★★★ T: 965 161 300, *www.hotelessidi.es*

Castilla Alicante ★★★ T: 965 151 001, *www.alicantehotelcastilla.com*

Tryp Ciudad de Alicante, T: 965 210 700

Cervantes, T: 965 209 822

La Florida Youth Hostel, T: 902 225 552, *www.ivaj.es*

Tourist Information

www.alicanteturismo.com, T: 965 929 802

Busot

Busot is a small town, of around 2600, north of the N-340 between San Juan and Jijona. You take the CV773 in order to get there and further on, at the end of this road - you come to Cuevas de Canelobre. Anyone interested in caverns will enjoy this place and it appears to have quite a presence as a venue for music and folk concerts. There is a massive display of stalagmites and stalactites in this highest vault in the whole of Spain, at 700m. *www.cuevasdecanelobre.com* T: 965 699 250

Cabezo D'Oro is the highest peak in the Sierra here. The apparent reference to oro (gold) is more likely to be connected with the Moorish word Ur for water which flowed into the Canelobre.

<u>Tourist Information</u>
www.ebusot.com, T: 965 699 092

El Campello

A fishing town 20 minutes by tram from Alicante with a bustling fish market and busy harbour, El Campello has over 23,000 inhabitants. The influx of tourism is probably a real threat to the old fishing industry.

The town is the main resort at the northern edge of Alicante city (13km). The centre of the old town is located 2km from the coast on a small hill whilst the main tourist area is built around the former fishing district with plenty of amenities, including El Campello yacht club.

El Campello has a varied and attractive coastline of 23km in length. At the extreme north, next to the Coveta Fuma, there are cliffs and small coves of sand, gravel and rocks with clear water that are well-known nudist beaches.

The town has a supermarket, shops, bars, restaurants, estate agents, banks and children's play area. A street market is held on Wednesdays in the town.

It holds its Moros y Cristianos Fiesta during October each year where the mock battles and parades are held throughout the town. As ever the colourful evening parades with spectacular costumes end with the inevitable fireworks.

El Campello's tower (built in the 1500s) overlooking the marina was originally used as a lookout for pirates. Fires were lit to warn other towers along the coast of the pirate's approach.

Bonalba Golf Club is a couple of minutes away.

Places To Stay
Pueblo Acantilado ★ ★ ★ ★ T: 965 638 146, *www.hotelpuebloacantilado.com*

Jorge I ★ ★ ★ T: 965 635 830, *www.hoteljorge1.net*

Mar Azul, T: 965 635 588, *www.hotel-marazul.com*

San Juan, T: 965 652 308, *www.hsanjuan.es*

Els Picalons, T: 965 699 454

Tourist Information
www.elcampello.es, T: 965 634 606

Jijona/Xixona
Jijona is the birthplace of turrón, a famous Spanish sweet made with almonds and honey. There are numerous roadside stalls where it is sold with pots of honey and even a turrón museum where you can see how it is produced. *www.museodelturron.com* T: 965 610 225

The mountains of the Font Roja Natural Park can be seen from the town, where there are beehives that were originally used by the Moors to collect the honey to make turrón.

Places To Stay
Pou de la Neu, 2*, T: 667 531 023, *www.poudelaneu.com*

Tourist Information
www.xixona.es, T: 965 610 300

Los Arenales del Sol

Just 8km south of Alicante city this resort boasts gorgeous sandy beaches and clear water and is an ideal place to relax in the sun. There are numerous bars, restaurants, shops, gift stores and apartments to rent. Los Arenales is ideally located just a couple of kilometres from the airport. El Plantio golf club is 5km away.

Muchamiel/Mutxamel

Muchamiel is close to Alicante and San Vicente with a population of 1200. It used to be a summer resort for the residents of Alicante and is an interesting village, surrounded by canals and irrigation tunnels. The parish church has a 14th century gothic tower.

There is a private airfield open to all general aviation.

Alicante and Bonalba Golf Club are less than 10 minutes away.

Places To Stay
Bon Any, T: 619 001 948

San Juan de Alicante

San Juan de Alicante boasts a 7km beach that is often described as one of the best in Spain. Accordingly, the tourist industry here is thriving, bars, hotels and restaurants dominate the seafront and a there is a golf course nearby, should anyone need a break from relaxing on the sand.

There are three small coves that aren't easy to get to and have therefore been designated as naturist beaches.

The town itself is worthy of interest. It has a seventeenth century parish church and three hermitages. Nearby is the Santa Faz monastery. A street market is held at San Juan on Saturdays.

It is 15km to Al Altet airport.

Alicante Golf Club is adjacent to San Juan (Partido).

Places To Stay
Hesperia Alicante Golf & Spa ★★★★★ T: 965 235 000, *www.hesperia.com*

Husa Villa San Juan, T: 965 653 954

Torre Sant Joan, T: 965 940 973

Abril, T: 965 653 408, *www.motelabril.com*

Tourist Information
www.santjoandalacant.es, T: 965 653 245

San Vicente del Raspeig

This is a large industrial town where the University of Alicante is situated and on the outskirts of Alicante city, part of the same conurbation. Approximately 30,000 students attend the college and consequently the town is home to a number of foreign residents although the majority of the population is Spanish.

San Vicente is a modern city, much of the residential development has occurred over the last fifty years in tandem with industrial expansion. Its street market is held on Saturdays.

Tourist Information
www.raspeig.es, T: 965 672 670

CASE STUDY
Colin Wiffen from Norfolk owns an apartment in Guardamar del Segura
www.costablancaholiday.info
www.grabapig.com

We decided to start looking to buy abroad because we love sunshine and didn't feel that we liked the direction in which Britain is moving! Spain is a great country with (mostly) very friendly people, a relaxed atmosphere and a strong sense of family.

We are still in the UK building towards our future plans. In the meantime we rent our apartment. Many people who are thinking of buying in the area have rented it out and found it a nice base and a useful location. This doesn't pay the mortgage in full but every bit is a help. This may be the way forward for other people if they do not want to move just yet.

We went to Guardamar del Segura to check it out as friends have an apartment there. The first day I arrived I hated it, the next I loved it, truly it happened that quick. We came back 6 months later to start looking to buy and when we drove into Guardamar it felt like we were driving home.

We bought an apartment in a residential complex. There are 33 dwellings of which the majority (except about 5) are owned by Spanish. The Spanish can be quite noisy and can do a lot of Furniture rearranging (scraping on the floor) but we are lucky, and our neighbours seem very nice. We always speak in Spanish where possible as most do not speak English (our Spanish is not perfect but always appreciated).

What's the best thing about where I live? Everything is great here; the location (views to the sea), the cuisine (a diversity of different restaurants), the locals (most are very friendly), the town (still predominantly Spanish so unspoiled by an over abundance of British bars and fish and chip shops).

It is essential to be able to speak Spanish. Think to how you feel when foreigners in the UK don't speak English! It is always appreciated and it enables you to mix with locals, buy from local shops, use local tradesmen and enriches your life. Don't be embarrassed about using it, my philosophy is that if the person you are speaking to cannot speak English, even your poor Spanish is one step better towards communication. Just remember, you are the foreigner!

Some Spanish officials (such as those who manage our community) can be very poor with communicating with the British, just remember that some may have the same opinion of foreigners (us) that some people have in the UK.

My Advice:

1. Do your research, don't buy a house or apartment in any country without exercising the same logic and common sense that you would in the UK.

2. Do not buy a property thinking it will make you rich, there are still a large number of empty properties, see it as a long term investment and you won't lose out.

3. We found our own Lawyer, never (in my opinion) use the lawyer of the company selling you the house; it just doesn't make any sense! We got caught on our first purchase attempt and had to take the developer to court, we won because we had good legal representation and were in the right.

4. The bottom line, don't trust anybody however nice they seem when they stand to gain from telling you what you want to hear. Buying a property is a big decision to take, a wise step to make, but just go in with your eyes open and get your legal representative to do all necessary searches etc, it is worth the extra cost.

5. Don't burn your bridges! If you can afford it, never sell your house in the UK (or your home country). I have known too many people who sell up, a year or two later they don't like it and then they cannot get back on the property ladder back home.

6. It is better to go for a year and pay rent, this should be long enough to see if you like it or not.

Currently my plan is to retire out to Spain, I have no desire to be working full time for somebody else by the time I am 55. Life is for living. A risk is always worth taking if it is a calculated one, there is no advancement without risk in my opinion.

BAJO VINALOPÓ

Crevillent

Crevillent is very Moorish in character. Its main industry has been the manufacture of carpets, initially starting with esparto grass carpets. The Romans named it Campus Spartarius.

Crevillent went on to have a chequered history similar to Albatera, being pushed around by various forces. In the early 17th century Crevillent consisted of 400 families the majority being Moorish. It was at least another 100 years before it began to stabilise and develop as we know it today.

Now with a population of over 28,000 Crevillent has a Catholic Church called *Mare de Déu de Betlem*, a museum dedicated to Valencian art and an archaeological museum.

Of interest, Jaume was a bearded highwayman in the Crevillent region, the equivalent of the British Robin Hood figure. He finally got put to death in Murcia.

Places To Stay
Goya, T: 965 401 550

Tourist Information
www.crevillent.es, T: 965 401 526

El Altet

El Altet is generally associated with the ever-growing Alicante airport and usually people are buzzing in and out by all means possible. However it has a number of other interesting things going for it worth mentioning. It actually has very fine weather which of course is one of the reasons for putting the airport here in the first place. The beach is of extreme ecological interest as it is backed by sand dunes. So fine sandy beaches to boot...

The fiesta in El Altet is celebrated for Saint Francis of Assisi in August.

Close to El Altet is the Ciudad de la Luz created in 2004 and completed in 2008 - a major audio visual centre with top rate facilities for making all sorts of cinematic and video productions.

Elche (Elx)

The capital of the Baix Vinalopó, Elche is famous for its forest of date palms, three hundred thousand of which surround the city, originally planted by the Moors in the 10th Century. The city was built on the banks of the Vinalopó River and a dam was built in 1632 to allow irrigation in the surrounding farmlands. Elche is a thriving city with a rich history.

Spain's most famous piece of ancient art, the stone bust of an Iberian priestess known as La Dama d'Elx dating from 5BC was found nearby. The original is now on display at the National Museum of Archaeology in Madrid, although there is an exact replica in the city. Greek, Roman and Moorish artefacts have also been found in the area.

The old city has a number of buildings worthy of interest including the Altamira Palace, the Basilica of Santa Maria, the Moorish fortress and the Moorish baths. All over the city you will find buildings with elaborate stonework as well as numerous statues and monuments. The best views of the city can be taken in from the banks of the Vinalopó.

Elche's palm trees, to be found everywhere, give the city an exotic flavour. The Palmerar d'Elche is a forest of over 200,000 palm trees. This impressive park was declared a World Heritage Site in the year 2000, frequently described as an oasis in al-andalus.

In the Huerto del Cura – the Priest's Garden – stands an unusual palm known as the Imperial Palm, notable for its seven arms. A miniature train ride can be taken through the palm grove that surrounds the city.

Within the Huerto del Cura is a recommended restaurant "Els Capellans" specialising in all mediterranean foods but is probably a friendly plastic card job. However I am ready to give it a go on my next visit as I realise that it is too long since my last visit.

Around Elche is a large agricultural area where farmhouses and bungalows are scattered amongst cultivated land. An important nature reserve at the Laguna del Hondo, is a few kilometres from the town and north of the salt pans of Santa Pola.

Elche is famous for its mystery play, El Misteri d'Elx, that takes place each 14th and 15th of August and attracts a number of visitors to the city. The play is performed in the basilica of Santa Maria and is supposed to have been performed every year since the thirteenth century. The drama tells the story of the death, assumption and coronation of the Virgin Mary and is performed by local amateur men and boys.

Elche is the third largest city in the Valencia region with a population of 300,000. It has all the amenities you would expect to find in a large city and is located very close to Alicante Airport making the local conference centre (Ciutat d'Elx) easily accessible to international business visitors.

The main fiesta (August 13th) is called Nit de l'Albà (Night of the Dawn) in which the night sky is set on fire with a city-wide fireworks display which lasts into the early hours.

The three things to buy from Elche are dates, lace and shoes.

A street market is held on Monday and Saturday, and on Sundays there is a craft market in the Plaza de Raval.

Rio Safari park on the Elche-Santa Pola road is a great place to take the kids, with various animals, dolphin displays, swimming pools and water slides.

The city has an Archaeological Museum (MAHE), a Palaeontological Museum and Arab Baths to visit.

El Plantio Golf Club is a fifteen-minute drive away.

Places To Stay
Areca ★★★★ T: 965 685 477, *www.hotelareca.es*
AC Elche ★★★ T: 966 662 065, *www.ac-hotels.com*
Milenio ★★★ T: 966 612 033, *www.hotelmilenio.com*
Ibis ★★ T: 966 615 451
Madruga, T: 966 674 794
Tryp Ciudad de Elche, T: 966 610 033
Galicia, T: 965 419 182, *www.hostal-galicia.net*

Tourist Information
www.turismedelx.com, T: 966 658 140

Guardamar del Segura

Guardamar del Segura is backed by a large pine forest. The 11km long white sandy beach outlines 800 hectares of dunes covered by pine trees, eucalyptus and palm trees. The town derives its name from the Arabs name Guald-a-amar (River of the Sand). You can even have a camel ride!

Guardamar's local fiestas include L'Encantà, Fogueres de Sant Joan and Moros y Cristianos. A local drink to try is Aigua de València made from Cava, fresh orange juice and Cointreau.

Located at the mouth of the River Segura, Guardamar del Segura is another tourist honey pot.

Guardamar was originally situated further inland but after it was destroyed by the 1829 earthquake, the town was rebuilt closer to the coast.

The Dunas de Guardamar is a woodland park by the coast created at the end of the last century when rows of pine trees were planted to prevent the advancing sands from the beach encroaching on the town. The park is a lovely place to walk through, its fauna includes red squirrels and black swans.

There are plenty of beautiful, sandy beaches, backed by large stretches of sand dunes; the most popular are the Centro and Roqueta beaches whilst those next to the mouth of the river tend to be quieter.

The town is well developed and the beaches are backed by modern hotels and apartments, though the centre of the old town retains its original Spanish charm. Guardamar's population of 10,000 includes a large number of British expatriates. La Marquesa Golf Club is just 6km away.

Easily reached from Alicante, Guardamar is 23km from the airport, or 35km from Murcia's San Javier airport, linked by the main N-332 coast road.

The mouth of the River Seguro lies north of Guardamar

Guardamar has a mixture of international restaurants and typical Spanish bars as well as plenty of supermarkets supplying local produce and imported products from other European countries.

In the peak season there's a night market where you can pick up a great selection of arts and crafts. On Wednesday afternoons, the streets are transformed by the hustle and bustle of the weekly market and on Sundays the "rastra" (flea market) takes place.

Between Guardamar and Torrevieja there is a nudist beach, Los Tuseles.

Places To Stay
Parque Mar ★★★★ T: 966 725 172

Campomar ★★★ T: 965 728 000, *www.hotelesposeidon.com*

Guardamar ★★ T: 965 729 650, *www.hotelguardamar.com*

Las Dunas, T: 965 728 110

Levante, T: 965 727 346

Tourist Information
www.guardamar.net, T: 965 724 488

Colin Wiffen on Guardamar del Segura

There's a Sunday market nearby at Montesinos that sells just about everything. We always go to buy cooked chicken, fresh fruit and veg plus knickknacks and furniture. There are big supermarkets in town and near our apartment, Mas y Mas and Mercadona. Fresh prawns are fantastic and even Rioja at €2 tastes great.

Walking or cycling in The Parque Natural, can be done anytime, often you will see the Spanish early in the morning (if you are up) and the wildlife is excellent and the forest peaceful.

We have some of the best beaches on the Costa Blanca, around 14km of Blue Flag golden sandy beaches.

Guardamar is great for eating out everything from traditional Spanish, Italian, tapas, Chinese, Indian, Mexican and great bars. A Couple of worthy mention are "La Vuelta" and "El Bocito" but all are great.

Colin Wiffen
www.costablancaholiday.info

Santa Pola

A coastal fishing town which, despite a thriving tourist industry retains much of its real Spanish charm. Situated on a calm bay, protected from the wind by a headland and with six golden sandy beaches it is ideal for bathing, water sports and fishing.

You can buy fresh fish straight off the boats in the fishing port and on Saturday there is a market. Many people visit Santa Pola as a base for day trips by boat to the island of Tabarca just 5 nautical miles away.

Santa Pola is still an important producer of salt. The present day town sits on the ruins of roman Portus Illicitanus and there are a number of archaeological gems to be seen.

There are 15km of beaches to relax in the sun or you can enjoy a whole range of water sports at the well organised marina. The Santa Pola Nautical club is particularly good, offering rowing, sailing and a canoeing school. Diving is also popular due to the clear waters in this area. The town has a series of wide sandy beaches and several secluded coves, one of which is a naturist beach. The Gran Playa is the most popular beach.

An impressive 16th Century castle lies in the centre of the town, now used as a museum. The Plaza del Calvario, in one of the higher areas of the town and offers gorgeous panoramic views of the area.

In July you have the week long fiesta Bous a la Mar (Bulls at the Sea) if you like that sort of thing, where bulls are run down the main street (Marqués de Campo) and into the Mediterranean. The town's must-see fiesta (La Virgen de Loreto) is held between 1st and 8th September when the town comes to life with street parades.

This is an area of outstanding natural beauty although most people only see it as they drive between Alicante airport and Guardamar de Segura. This might explain how it retains its magic despite the large conurbations all around. It is a place that demands respect at any time of the year.

Avocets at sunrise in Santa Pola

A number of migratory birds including heron which spend winter in the natural reserve are attracted by the salt flats. You are most likely to see flamingos as you cut through the saltpans.

Santa Pola sits alongside the marvellous city of Elche and its palm forests so there are many diverse things for the Nativespainer to get out of this area.

There are plenty of restaurants (serving excellent fresh seafood), hotels, bars and shops and a lively nightlife scene during the summer.

Daily markets sell fish fresh off the boats. The rastra (flea market) held on Saturdays is a must for bargain hunters.

It is within easy reach of Alicante airport, situated just 8km away on the main N-332 coastal road and the city of Alicante is 18km away. El Plantio Golf Club is just past the airport, 10km away.

As you cross the salt pans of Santa Pola you cannot fail to see a large black model of a bull, one of a number throughout Spain which had been erected by Osborne Sherry and Brandy as a form of advertising 52 years ago. However legislation was passed in 1980s prohibiting all forms of advertising on the motorways (Good decision!). The decision to bring the bulls down met with such protest that the Osborne Bull was deemed to be a "National Treasure" and has consequently survived to the present day.

The Cabo de Santa Pola, the headland next to Santa Pola is a nature reserve that is formed from fossilized coral reef, rising to 100 metres above the sea. Due to its height, it has become a great place to paraglide and hang glide.

If you look at much of the publicity and promotion for Santa Pola and the salt lakes there are numerous mentions of albatrosses. I'm afraid not. In the same way that one swallow does not a summer make this is a fallacy possibly based on an accident. It is likely that what people see are gannets as they are very close in size to the black browed albatross. All the research I have done showed that most albatrosses are confined to the southern oceans and a couple of smaller ones are to be found in the Atlantic. Thanks to Lisa Stuart and John from the Iberia Nature Forum for the expert advice (*www.iberianatureforum.com*).

Places To Stay

JM Santa Pola ★★★ T: 965 411 312,
www.jmhoteles.com

Pola-Mar ★★★ T: 965 413 200

Patilla ★★ T: 965 411 015, *www.hotelpatilla.com*

Quatre Llunes, T: 966 696 080,
www.hostalquatrellunes.com

Tourist Information

www.turismosantapola.es, T: 902 510 590

Las Salinas at Santa Pola

Tabarca

With a population of just 98 Tabarca is the largest of a group of islets which includes La Galera, La Nao and La Cantera. Several boats connect Tabarca with Alicante, Torrevieja and Santa Pola (5 nautical miles) and it makes a popular day trip destination. Visit *www.islatabarca.com* for ferry details.

Whilst researching I saw some pretty negative comments about Tabarca. I can only say one person's load of old dirty rocks is another person's heaven. The fact that boats are running all day from Santa Pola would I have thought indicate that a lot of people think it is an interesting day out, of which my son and I are two. And another major factor is there are no cars!

Best known for its marine reserve this completely flat and tiny island (1750m x 300m) is also worth a visit for its church, lighthouse and the old fort walls on the western side of the island. As well as being an officially protected marine reserve it is also an EU zone for the protection of birds.

The completely flat Tarbarca Island measures just 1750m x 300m

Snorkelling, diving in a little yellow submarine, or taking a ride in a glass-bottomed boat which reveals the rich marine life below the waves are some of the experiences available. A must is to take lunch at one of the seafood restaurants for a perfect day in the sun on Isla de Tabarca.

Before 1700, the island was known as Isla de Sant Pau ("Saint Paul's Island") as it is believed to be the island where he disembarked from. Tabarca was a part of the republic of Genoa until 1741. It was overrun by Tunisians and Algerians for a while. However in 1760,

Carlos III ordered the fortification and re-population of the island to halt the practice of Barbary pirates using it as a base to attack the Levantine coast. The island became New Tabarca, named by Carlos III in 1768 after its Tunisian sister island. It was re-populated by Genovese fishermen who were taken to the island, jointly with a Spanish garrison. A military engineer Fernando Méndez Ras planned a fortified town and walls, with warehouses and houses.

In 1850 the governor and the garrison were removed. At the end of the 19th century, the island had a population of around 1000 people mainly devoted to fishing. The Governor's house is the only hotel on the island.

Tourist Information
www.turismosantapola.es, T: 902 510 590

CASE STUDY
Sharon Richards from the Midlands living in Albatera
www.livespainforlife.com

Fed up with the what life had to offer us in the UK knowing the business we had run for over 5 years with partners could not sustain two families forever we decided to move to Spain. It was more for the children than for us.

We left behind family and friends, which was the big wrench especially as my Mother had been diagnosed with breast cancer a few months prior to us leaving the UK. We had a lovely 4 bed home in a nice area and a good income (at the time), nice cars a very good social life. Oh and I had a very fit body, which is a distant memory and I am not talking about my husband (he came with me)! Courtesy of 3 kick boxing sessions and 3 gym sessions a week, but I have been so busy since I arrived there has been no time to get back into it. I do miss it especially when I wave (all you women will know what I am talking about!)

I am a relocator/property agent but basically match up people with property and help them with all the paperwork and issues that they wouldn't hear about. I run an up to date website with information and advice on as many aspects as you can imagine to do with the moving process. I keep clients past and present up to date with all the changes that there are here in Spain.

We started our search for a new home in a place called Mazzarón near Cartagena but inland. We initially bought a holiday home but we soon realized it wasn't suitable for long term living with children. We needed an International school where out eldest could do his A levels (he was too old to go to Spanish school).

We visited Spain several times and did lots of research. We visited both the International schools and the Spanish state school and looked for somewhere for the

131

children to carry on with their Martial Arts classes. We wanted somewhere very Spanish but well situated so everywhere we wanted to get to was easily accessible.

We now live in what's called a Spanish *finca* (a *finca* is a plot of land with a little house on it called an *almacen* or a*lbergue*). When we bought it, it was supposed to have been reformed, (anyone living here will know what we mean). It was reformed to a certain degree but not how we wanted it.

The house is situated in a little hamlet of about 10 other houses mainly Spanish weekend houses, all similar plots but different shapes and sizes. After 4 years of very hard work lots of dust and mess we have updated the property with all the mod cons we were used to in the UK like efficient electricity for starters (that's another story), telephone and internet access. The list is endless, but we now have a lovely 5-bedroomed and 5-bathroomed house, a new pool and a bar and terrace area.

We live in the countryside just 5 minutes from the town of Albatera with all its amenities, which include a 24-hour health centre, gym, indoor pool, shops supermarkets and restaurants, schools for all ages, football, music school etc. We are 15 minutes from the beautiful city of Elche, the city of the palms and 25 minutes to Alicante airport and 30 minutes to the coast of Guardamar and La Marina. We have a train station very close by which takes you in the direction of Murcia or Alicante. We have a mixture of neighbours both expats and Spanish. Everyone is friendly but the houses are set far enough apart to be private and no one really bothers anyone else too much unless there is a problem or there is a delivery of a box of the latest crop.

The views are superb of the mountains which surround our house, we hadn't realized at the time when we bought how lucky we were and how beautiful they were. The town is very Spanish still and unspoilt by the influx of foreigners, unlike the coast. However everyone is different and some people may disagree but for us we found what we had hoped for.

Sometimes I am sad that I don't have much free time and also its hard to go anywhere locally without being accosted with some question about some aspect of life here or help with some paperwork, even when I am trying to have a quiet time with my family or friends. However I have a thriving, successful business with a good name and this is the price I have to pay so I accept this.

I think it's very important that you can speak Spanish! I have to say I have been lucky as my children were fluent very quickly because all their friends are Spanish so they have helped me tremendously. I also have a fantastic solicitor who has helped my business but I have no doubt the more my Spanish improves so will my reputation. And that here is everything! In Albatera there are free Spanish lessons twice a week and next September there will be two levels as newcomers can find the classes a bit hard going. I have to say I have no regrets.

My tips for people thinking of coming to Spain:

1. Do your research. Come out on as many visits as you can manage, several times at least and speak to people.
2. Try to learn the language.
3. Don't have too many preconceived ideas.
4. Be prepared to work harder than you ever have before if you need to work to support your family.
5. Have at least a few years income behind you whilst you get established.
6. Most of all be realistic there is no help here financially if you do not work or don't have a home and have not paid into the system.

VEGA BAJA DEL SEGURA

Albatera

Albatera is a well laid out town with palms fringing the broad streets. It has a very interesting and varied historical past. Moorish in its origins it was re-conquered by Alfonso el Sabio in 1266 (King Alfonso X).

This small town is famed for the Baroque style door of the church. There are several other interesting corners to the Plaza including the town hall and casino.

The local fiesta is in honour of San Jaime.

Sitting on the Rio de Segura it has always had an agricultural economy from the days of the Moors. Relying heavily on citrus fruits and pomegranates these days it is more rounded in its economy with animal farming and the textile industry being very important as well.

The Parque del Huerta, the municipal park of Albatera is 30,000sqm of parkland consisting of palms and gardens laid out with water fountains and a place for musical events.

During the civil war there was a Republican labour camp here which later became a concentration camp where mainly French soldiers were held.

Places To Stay
Estación de Servicio Los Martínez, T: 965 487 001

Tourist Information
www.albatera.org, T: 965 485 000

Almoradí

Almoradí is a very pleasant town of around 18,000 inhabitants, known for its furniture making. It also has one of the best markets, filling all the streets around the town church and spacious square on Saturday mornings. Frequently you will find live music or dancing going on in front of the church.

I asked a local businessman I know where he eats around Almoradí. He suggested Bar/Restaurante el Cruce in Almoradí. This restaurant is very famous, in particular for a dish called Pava Borracha.

His description is very funny. When I speak to native Spanish it reduces my sense of self-consciousness about my verb endings. And his description of "drunken turkey" almost removes my desire to be vegetarian!

"...is in Almoradí (Restaurante el Cruce) is very famous they make the drank Turkey (la pava borracha) they drank the turkey with alcohol (wine or brandy) before sacrifice the bird and cook. It's fantastic, no?"

Many people say it is: Camino de Catral 156 03160 Almoradí (965700356).

Tourist Information
www.aytoalmoradi.com, T: 965 700 101

Benijófar

The chances are you have found yourself driving behind a very large lorry from Benijófar, as this small town is in the centre of the vegetable growing region of Alicante. Almost all these little places which were very much in the campo are being expanded at the edges.

More and more shops are appearing in tandem with this development. There is a good Indian restaurant as well as fish 'n chips and a Chinese, and a useful Dutch charcuterie. Many urbanisations are being developed in what were the lemon and orange groves. There is a small market on Tuesdays and an ace veterinary practice. Benijófar sits between the old town of Rojales and Ciudad Quesada.

Tourist Information
www.benijofar.org, T: 966 715 401

The famous baroque doorway of the the church dedicated to San Jaime built 1729

Catral

Part of the Vega Baja Catral dates back to the Arab conquest. It is deep campo and has flourished under the impact of Muslim agricultural traditions. Slowly the area is undergoing change as old fincas fall to development. However some illegally built houses have been demolished achieving some degree of notoriety.

The fiesta patronal is on the 24th June for St John The Baptist, with floats and parades. You can go hiking or cycling up to the El Hondo reservoir.

There is access to the railway nearby.

Places To Stay
Villa de Catral ★★★★ T: 966 787 876

Tourist Information
www.ayuntamientocatral.com, T: 965 723 000

Ciudad Quesada

Here's an interesting story of the family Quesada, I defer to my mother-in-law, Favel again.

Favel on Ciudad Quesada

Ciudad Quesada was at one time a huge area of land overlooking the salt lakes and owned by the Quesada family. They decided to sell off plots of land for building villas. The first villas built being those closest to the centre of the urbanisation. The plots were large and the villas impressive. I lived there for 16 years from 1990 and I enjoyed every minute of it – it was a grand place to live.

It is now in effect a town with many shops and restaurants serving international cuisine rather than Spanish bars and cafes. Banks and estate agents also abound. The Aqua Park opens for business in the

---

summer months. It has its own ayuntamiento, fire station and public and private health clinics.

The nearest beach is a 10-15 minute drive away. Rojales and many smaller villages lie nearby. There are great views of the surrounding mountains.

Nowadays, however I feel too much building has happened, with the villas on smaller plots of land and many in terrace form and the whole estate sprawling further and further into the campo and now reaching the edge of the natural park. And consequently spoilt in my opinion.

Papa Quesada, Pepita his daughter and Justo his son still live in the centre in enormous houses of course. There is in fact a statue of him near the golf course. When I first went to live there Quesada had its own little aerodrome – all houses now.

Dolores

Dolores is a town in the heart of Segura Huerta, inland from the Costa Blanca and is 10km from the beaches of La Marina and Guardamar and approximately 20 minutes from the airport.

Dolores has a great open-air market every Friday morning where you can buy locally grown fruit and veg such as watermelons, oranges, artichokes, beans and apricots. Not forgetting clothes and textiles.

Agriculture is a major industry for the region, along with tourism. Property prices in Dolores are much lower than on the coast and the approval of a large housing development with a golf course attracts many overseas buyers looking for a bargain property by the Costa Blanca. There is a large contingent of foreign nationals living in Dolores.

Dolores' most important fiestas are the Feria de Agosto and the Fiesta de la Virgen de los Dolores held in the middle of September. The Feria de Agosto (August Fair, held in August unsurprisingly) features a large Spanish Horse Contest where well over a thousand horses are shown as well as cattle and dogs.

Tourist Information
www.aytodolores.es, T: 965 726 025

Los Montesinos

Los Montesinos lies between Torrevieja and Guardamar, behind the salt lakes. It's a fairly small town with 2800 inhabitants.

Still part of the campo, just, with surrounding market gardens and orange groves and the salt lakes close by. Agriculture is still an important part of the town, but tourism is on the increase. Its market is held every Friday evening.

Club de Golf La Finca is a few kilometres away and La Marquesa Golf Club is a 15-minute drive away.

The town is 35km from San Javier airport and 42km from Alicante airport.

Places To Stay
La Torre ★★★ T: 966 720 073,
www.hotelrestaurantelatorre.com

Tourist Information
www.losmontesinos.es, T: 966 721 087

Orihuela

The city lies at the foot of a sierra with the Río Segura flowing through the city on its way to Guardamar. There are some architectural gems in the old city where superb churches and buildings of Baroque, Gothic and Renaissance origin can be seen.

Above the town is the Monastery. A very hard walk up to then find that women are not permitted inside! The Santiago church is the building where the Catholic Monarchs held a general parliament in 1488 in order to generate funds to finance the movement that was to culminate in the conquest of Granada in 1492.

A custom unique to Orihuela can be seen at the Burial Procession at Easter, when one of the procession's floats contains a representation of the "Diablesa" – the female form of the devil. There is also a statue of the Diablesa in the town.

El Palmeral just on the approach to Orihuela is the second largest palm forest in Spain and is worthy of time being spent here too.

The town has all the amenities you would expect from a town of 56,000 people, including an excellent hospital, and a good selection of shops, banks and supermarkets. Market day is Tuesday.

Club de Golf las Ramblas de Orihuela. La Finca Algorfa Golf Club is 18km away.

Orihuela is easily accessible, situated inland on the N-340, 5km from the A-7, the motorway that runs between Murcia and Alicante. It is 22km from Murcia and 59km from Alicante. San Javier airport is 38km away.

Rather weirdly the Orihuela Playa is actually at Cabo Roig, separated from the town geographically (which used to confuse the heck out of me when I first arrived and was trying to make sense of road signs).

Cabo Roig (Playa de Orihuela) is part of a favoured piece of coast line. When this area started to be developed it was pretty exclusive. People take for granted el Torre itself. It was a watchtower and part of a series along the coast probably Moorish in its origins and used up until the 17th century. Damaged by the earthquake of 1829 it is still an important historical building.

Lomas del Mar is a residential complex with a private gated road and all types of services available. Supermarkets, banks, cafes and restaurants are nearby. It is near to the beaches of Mil Palmeras, Playa Flamenca, La Zenia, Cabo Roig and Punta Prima. There are communal swimming pools nearby and cycling, diving, fishing, golf, horse-riding, mountain-biking, sailing, swimming, tennis, walking and wind-surfing amongst the many facilities.

Dehesa de Campoamor is an urbanisation close to Orihuela playa, developed around a series of coves and headlands. It has much charm and a pretty, busy marina as well.

Places To Stay
Meliá Boutique Palacio de Tudemir ★★★★ T: 966 738 010

La Zenia ★★★★ T: 966 760 200

Rey Teodomiro, T: 966 743 348

Lo Soto, T: 676 963 515, *www.losoto.com*

Tourist Information
www.orihuelaturistica.es, T: 965 304 645

Pilar de la Horadada

This is the most southern town of the Valencian Community and hence the province of Alicante. The Torre de la Horadada built in the 16th century had been used as the usual watchtower for the coast. The marina has a good number of moorings and the beaches are very well cared for with clear water.

My friend Jackie who lived close to this area for nearly two years offers her personal view.

Jackie On Pilar de la Horadada

A pleasant and airy town with the coastline five minutes away and with an easy route inland through pine forests and hills. The A-7 motorway is a good alternative to the N-332 for driving to Torrevieja or Alicante as the coastal strip from Pilar de la Horadada to Torrevieja passes through the very busy route via Cabo Roig and the urbanisations on both sides of the road.

Pilar de la Horadada has a good selection of shops, supermarkets, bars and restaurants including three Chinese and two Indian restaurants. Competition leads to good value and offers for instance cheaper, early evening meals.

Both holiday and residential areas for Spanish people and expats mean coastal and inland there are large developments, with a new golf course on the outskirts of Pilar de la Horadada (on the road to Orihuela). These developments bring the inevitable construction industry and retail outlets with several bricolage/ferreterias, furniture and garden shops and so on.

English is widely spoken and there is an excellent and well attended cinema with films in English (and Spanish subtitles) at weekends. Two showings each on both Saturday and Sunday throughout the year except

---

August. A good selection of films are shown in this Spanish run cinema with questionnaires for the public to ensure a good variety of films for all tastes.

"An excellent restaurant is situated about 20 minutes from Pilar de la Horadada and half way to San Miguel de Salinas, the Rebate Restaurant in the pine forests. (Finca Rebate, Ctra CV 952, km10.5, Pilar de la Horadada. T: 965-368-229.) Drive out past the established urbanisation of Campoverde toward Orihuela. This Spanish owned restaurant is a converted finca with a large outside terrace and views of the pine hills and the well tended grounds. The grounds have a chapel, water feature, a large duck pond with an island and an ostrich and emu in a large pen.

The Salt workings and lake are well signed and is an interesting area for wildlife including flamingoes. Along the coast from Torre de la Horadada is another wildlife area of interest at El Mojon. The sand dunes heading toward San Pedro del Pinatar are protected and the salt lakes here have walkways allowing one to watch the birdlife and beautiful views over the sea.

Places To Stay
La Horadada, T: 966 769 057

Congra, T: 965 352 101

Monte, T: 966 766 408

Tourist Information
www.pilardelahoradada.org, T: 966 767 068

Playa Flamenca

Playa Flamenca sits just north of La Zenia and is indeed part of a desirable location. It is is also on the new paseo that is being constructed between Campoamor and Torrevieja which can only enhance this particular area of the Costa. There is a large and very busy Saturday market on the main street.

San Isidro

San Isidro is near Albatera and actually sits on the railway line which serves the region. Just alongside the station signed Albatera-Catral is the old wooden station which could do with a bit of preservation. San Isidro is a neat little place with a pleasant looking piscina and enough amenities. As you head out towards Catral there is an advertisement for a rastro/boot sale.

Places To Stay
La Granadina ★ ★ ★ ★ T: 965 489 064, *www.ghihoteles.com*

San Miguel de Salinas

Is another agricultural town across the salt lake from Torrevieja, its main interest being its position on the shores of the lake. With a population of 4000, San Miguel offers plenty of shops, bars and supermarkets, with a Wednesday market. The amenities in Torrevieja are 12km away. The town's main fiesta is in October when they make a giant paella in the town square.

It is well positioned for several golf courses particularly Campoamor and Villamartin.

The town is 30km from San Javier airport and 38km from Alicante airport. It is located about 5km off the main N-332 coastal road.

Jackie On San Miguel

San Miguel de Salinas has a main street lined with orange trees and open country views, a beautiful church square with fountains and trees full of parakeets. Again new and older developments have brought increased numbers of foreigners into the area. On my first visit I stepped out of the car beside a group of chattering English women and it sounded like an English market town on a Saturday morning.

Considered by many expat residents to be an up-market area, San Miguel has good bars and restaurants but with the ever-growing development and increasing population growth especially around Los Balcones, driving can be slow.

Margaret on San Miguel

Personally I am not that keen on restaurants, preferring to go out in the daytime and come home to a nice bit of fish on the balcony chez nous. However, we do go to the Indian restaurant at Punta Prima. You have to book or you never get a place. We also like our little Chinese in Los Balcones. There are in fact two and both are nice, but the older one up the hill from the supermarket is very friendly. The people are local (resident Brit mostly), everyone is enjoying him/herself and looking brown, healthy and happy for the most part. That perhaps is the difference between people in England, especially of a similar income, and Spain. The quality of life there is better for them, money goes further, the weather is kinder and the atmosphere is friendly.

Our apartment in Lago Jardín 1 is off the busy San Miguel - Torrevieja Road next to Los Balcones. It is a complex of two-floor apartments with absolutely dismal sound insulation. Fortunately there is often no one upstairs. Since people live at close quarters with open terraces, everybody gives one the time of day or has a chat and people there are generally friendly and caring. When someone has a serious problem the neighbours will help, even giving money-raising fêtes to make a contribution to care, repatriation, etc. It's mostly Brits, but there are Spanish, Norwegian, French and others as well.

Our favourite beach is Cabo Roig and in fact it is so pleasant and picturesque that we rarely go elsewhere. There are two small roads leading to it where you can park and there is a fairly steep walk to the beach down the cliffs which surround it. It is a very pretty bay with views beyond, a yachting harbour at the side and a beach café with chairs and parasols. Many Spanish, Germans and of course the ubiquitous Brits use it. The bay is very protected from the wind and in fact it is often calm when other bays – for example La Zenia – are windy and the sea rough. Campoamour is another, larger beach which is very clean and pleasant and, if one likes to go to town, the small Playa del Cura in Torrevieja is also nice, but I guess it gets very busy in high summer.

We usually walk around the coast at Punta Prima going south towards La Zenia. There is a very well-placed restaurant with good tapas right on the coast called the Nautilus where one can while away the time and gaze at that marvellous blue of the sea in Spain which laps against the rocks there. Also, the walk from the Hotel Zenia to Cabo Roig and back is a very picturesque one around a path in the rocks. Another pleasant one is around the coast from the Playa del Cura northwards in Torrevieja.

We like the San Miguel market on a Wednesday. It is cosy and not too big and one can pass by the shops on the way: the fish shop, the ferretería, etc. It also has flowers which are not found in all markets. Oh the joys of the Spanish ironmongers. They seem to sell everything from paint to bottle openers to loose nuts and bolts. The one in Punta Prima is very welcoming and the staff are multilingual – useful sometimes for more complicated problems. The market of Playa Flamenco is really huge and one has to walk miles to see it all. The market in Guardamar del Segura is also very large and the town is small and pleasant to look around.

If you want a laugh, you have only to go to the enormous complex of Villamartin. The eateries and the bars are all in a large building on two floors and the behaviour of some – or most – of the young people in the bars makes one feel out of touch and very old. Bald heads and tight jeans for the men and low-cut dresses with boobs spilling out on to tables for the young women was de rigueur. A place to avoid!

Margaret and her partner are long time residents of Geneva and have a tiny little place in Lago Jardin 1.

Places To Stay
Casa Pilar, T: 966 705 984

Tourist Information
T: 965 720 001

Torrevieja

Originally a salt-mining and fishing village, due to its location between the sea and two large salt lakes (Las Salinas), in recent years it has become an extremely popular destination for visitors and expats from the UK and northern Europe.

There have been massive changes in the time I have known it. Semana Santa Casino Development along the coast has slowly improved the beach, although to the north of the town the beach is quite rocky in parts. Please note if you are wise you will avail yourself of the underground parking in front of the Casino, which is worth finding in its own right for the Moorish canopy. It's also an excellent spot for taking a coffee or a beer, for people watching, or eating an icecream in the evening.

Around the corner from the Casino is the Pizza Nostra, are probably the best pizzas I have eaten outside of Italy. There is a second Pizza Nostra on the N-322 toward La Zenia but this one hasn't been tested yet. Spanish people (and me) queue up for a table here. This is where the Spanish come to their apartments for their holiday in August. The town has a Palacio de la Musica with a coffee bar beneath. It's worth checking what's on at *www.unionmusicaltorrejense.org*

In the evenings especially on Sundays the local Spanish people "dar un paseo" (promenade) and they will be wearing their very best and usually beautiful clothes.

Torrevieja is located 27km from Murcia's San Javier airport and 34km from Alicante airport on the main N-332 coast road and this helps to make it a popular year-round holiday destination. It is difficult to believe that 200 years ago, there was only an old watch tower (Torre vieja) and a couple of houses.

The salt flats behind led to the rapid development of the town and port. Today it is the biggest producer of salt in Europe. The salt-water lakes absorb water from the atmosphere and create a special micro-climate which is widely regarded to be beneficial for sufferers of rheumatism, asthma, bronchitis and other respiratory problems. The salt lakes are now a nature reserve, attracting a diverse range of migratory and nesting birds.

The Museum of the Sea and Salt will help explain Torrevieja's past but it also has many interesting maritime pieces of history like the Delfin S-61 submarine given by the Ministry of Defence to Torrevieja. The "Pascual Flores" the last of the old coastal fishing boats of Torrevieja is being restored at the Salt Quay.

There is a huge variety of Spanish and international restaurants as well as historic sites worthy of interest including the town's casino.

Playa La Mata - Torrevieja

A number of golf courses are within easy reach, Villamartin being the closest, 8km away. Las Ramblas, golf course known as the Royal at Campoamor lies in spectacular pine forests and is worth a visit even if you do not play golf.

There is a wide range of shops in Torrevieja, a few of them specializing in British and German goods. A huge street market takes place every Friday. You can buy anything from clothes and jewellery to Spanish handicrafts and local fresh produce.

In the town centre you'll find an indoor market selling a mind-boggling range of seafood straight off the boats at very cheap prices. There is also a daily seafront market with stalls displaying clothes and leather goods.

There are plenty of sporting facilities including sailing schools and diving clubs, horse riding stables, tennis courts and gymnasiums.

Torrevieja also has a large harbour for private yachts where small sightseeing boats offer cruises around the coastline and trips to the nearby island of Tabarca. Torrevieja's nearest passenger port offering services to the Balearics is in Alicante.

Amongst Torrevieja's tourist attractions is Iglesia Arciprestal de la Inmaculada Concepción which was originally built in 1789 but following a devastating earthquake in 1829 was reconstructed in 1844 using stones from the original Torre Vieja.

Las Salinas (the famous salt lakes to the west of the city), Paraje Natural Municipal Molino Del Agua (a hidden gem of a natural park) and Parque de las Naciones are all worth visiting for nature lovers.

For beach lovers there is 20km of coastline containing six large beaches - Cabo Cervera, El Cura, Los Locos, La Mata, Los Náufragos and Ferris.

The world-famous Habaneras festival for choral groups is held in late July and you can get full details at *www.habaneras.org*. During this period the city's population increases ten fold.

Torrevieja has the largest number of British residents of all the Spanish municipalities not to mention a growing community of Germans and Scandinavians, many of whom live there throughout the year. There are now over 160 nationalities represented on the padrón (electoral role). However it is Nils Gäbel a Swede, who really put Torrevieja on the tourist map. He saw its potential as a lovely place to live back in 1963. Not surprisingly there is a monument erected in his honour in the gardens of Torre del Moro.

Places To Stay

Cabo Cervera ★★★ T: 966 921 711,
www.hotelcabocervera.com

Masa Internacional ★★★ T: 966 921 537,
www.hotelmasa.com

Torrejoven ★★★ T: 965 707 145

Juan Carlos ★ T: 965 716 969, *www.hoteljuancarlos.com*

Lloyds Club, T: 966 920 000

Atlas, T: 965 705 555

Tourist Information

www.e-torrevieja.com, T: 965 715 936

Rojales

Rojales has the River Segura running straight through the middle of it which explains why it used to be a traditional farming village. The demands of the tourist industry on the coast have caused it to expand and it is now a town with a large sports hall, a theatre and large residential areas for people working in the service sector. A couple of kilometres from Rojales is the village of Benijófar. Both towns have attracted a large expatriate community but despite this they are still Spanish in character and are much quieter than nearby Torrevieja and Guardamar.

Rojales sits in the centre of a number of little hamlets still heavily involved in market gardening. Old Rojales is set in the caves abutting the back of what is now known as Ciudad Quesada.

A Rojales house front

Every first Sunday of the month the cave house area of Rojales holds an artisan's market. Many of the caves at the top are simply laid out with pristine white walls and ethnic style lights and several are workshops (I used to buy my Christmas presents here and the odd pressie for myself) and art galleries. One cave in particular is a bar serving Alhambra Reserva 1925 normally drunk straight out of the bottle. This is where I overcame my lady like reluctance to do this. Warning - this beer is 6.4%. There is also a cafe with music often featuring.

Rojales has plenty of shops and supermarkets catering to the needs of expatriates, an indoor market, and frequently overlooked, a little archaeological museum in the centre of the town. Amenities include a 24-hour filling station, an internet café and an international pub. The services offered by Torrevieja and Guardamar are a 20-minute drive away.

Rojales holds a market every Thursday.

La Finca Algorfa and La Marquesa Golf Clubs are a few minutes drive away. The towns are within easy reach of airports, Alicante's being 29km away and Murcia's 35km.

Main roads ensure that Benijófar and Rojales are easily accessible, well connected with both the coastal towns of the Costa Blanca as well as inland Vega Baja.

Places To Stay
Laguna Spa & Golf ★★★★ T: 965 725 577, www.hotellalaguna.com

El Corazón, T: 966 713 957

Tourist Information
T: 966 715 001

CASE STUDY
Steve Hall from Manchester, living in Torrevieja
www.thisisspain.info

My best bit of advice for people thinking about moving to Spain is to LEARN Spanish. This is vital, there's nothing more to add.

I had been a regular visitor to Spain over 30 years and I always knew I would come to stay. I have lived for 7 years on the Costa Blanca and it suits me perfectly. I thought about other regions but decided against them. Almería and the Costa de La Luz are not really developed enough and the Costa del Sol is too expensive and too expat. At the Costa Brava there are the language issues. In Galicia the weather! Madrid is too hot in summer and too cold and wet in winter. And of course, in Barcelona there's no decent football to watch!

I live in a detached villa and I don't really see anything of the "neighbours" but everybody seems to get on fine. The best thing about living here is the wireless internet as I work online and am active in many expat networks.

The biggest single mistake people make when coming here is not doing enough (or any!) homework before they arrive.

I love tapas, paella, fresh fish, fruit and veg and eating in GOOD Indian restaurants. I always love the genuine Spanish markets, not expat car-boots. Spanish TV is almost uniformly appalling. Sometimes it is so bad you can laugh at it - sometimes you just laugh with it.

I decided to come here for primarily health-reasons. The Spanish health service is MAGNIFICENT. I have some health challenges and I have pretty extensive knowledge of the local state hospitals. I have always found the speed and quality of care to be excellent. The attention to detail is impressive as is the condition/cleanliness of the hospitals and health centres.

Life is perfect except for the mosquitoes in the evening! My only regret is that I did not come here when I was younger. I intend to stay here in Torrevieja until I have an appointment 6 feet under.

Essential Information

EMERGENCY NUMBERS

112 Emergency Number for Police,
Fire Brigade & Ambulance

NON-EMERGENCY NUMBERS

091 National Police

092 Local Police

092 Guardia Civil

080 Fire Brigade

061 Ambulance

INTERNATIONAL DIALLING CODES

+34 Spain

+44 UK

HEALTH

Make sure you bring your European Health Insurance Card (EHIC) (previously E111) with you if you are visiting Spain. This allows you to receive limited treatment for reciprocal EU health cover arrangements while visiting Spain for less than six months in any one year. You will need this and your passport if you require emergency treatment. The form for the EHIC can be obtained at UK post offices or online.

You will be required to resort to private health service care beyond a certain point.

Remember the pharmacists within the 'farmacias' are very skilled and many more medicines can be bought over the counter than in UK (and frequently more cheaply.)

Dangers of the Sun

The most likely medical problems are sunburn and hangovers!

Beware heat stroke/sun stroke. This can be a life threatening condition at its worst and really unpleasant at best. I know from personal experience of trying to do too much climbing in the middle of the day with no reserve water, and touring the Alhambra around noon in August. I also once had to call the emergency doctor out to treat my partner after a very long hot day at a wedding. He had only had three pints of lager all day but was not making up lost fluids – and that was in England!

If you or members of your family become ill due to heatstroke you may well vomit and feel severely ill with a headache. It is probably wise to carry some salty biscuits and always carry water. If someone is suffering from heatstroke get them out of the sun preferably into a cool environment. Help the skin to cool down in any way you can. If worried get the person to a doctor or hospital straight away as they may well need an intravenous drip.

Please note a sensible nativespainer is watching what the locals are doing – not roasting themselves in the middle of the day. In fact very often the Spanish don't go down to the sea until early evening and then party around the beach until the sun has well and truly gone.

All that aside, Spain has nearly 40,000 diagnoses of skin cancer each year. Children are the most vulnerable as the effects of sunbathing for young children are accumulative in their effects for the risk of malignant melanoma.

Centros de Salud – Health Centres

Most towns have local clinics or Health Centres which can often be a first port of call:

Altea, C/ Galotxa, Garganes Basseta, T: 966 880 106

Benissa, Avda Ausias March, T: 965 732 461

Benidorm, Cl Tomás Ortuflo, T: 966 803 802

Calpe, Avda Conde de Altea, T: 965 835 011

Campello, C/ Convento, T: 965 632 536

Dénia, Avinguda Joan Fuster, T: 965 789 260

Javea, Plaza de la Constitucion, T: 965 792 500

Moraira. C/ Dr, Catalayud. T: 966 490 204

San Juan, C/ Ptda de Benali, T: 965 655 200

Teulad/Moraira, C/Dr Pitach, T: 965 741 136

Villajojosa C/ Juan Tonda Aragonés, T: 965 895 385

Hopitales - Hospitals

Alicante, Hospital General, Maestro Alonso, 109, T: 965 938 300

Dénia, Hospital Marina Alta (La Pedrera), Ptda real de Santa Paula, T: 965 787 012

Villajoyosa, Pla d'Aljuv, T: 966 859 800

Ambulance Services

Alicante T: 965 153 333

Benidorm T: 965 855 945

Calpe T: 965 838 266

Elche T: 965 443 773

La Nucia T: 966 873 828

DRIVING

Spain has strict drink driving laws only allowing 0.5 milligrams of alcohol per millilitre of blood - stricter than in the UK where the limit is 0.8.

Speeding and other traffic offences are subject to on-the-spot fines.

Ensure you do not cross the solid white line as you enter the motorway from a slip road, but wait until the line is broken.

Be sure to use your indicators overtaking and returning to the inside lane.

GB sticker: UK registered vehicles displaying Euro-plates (circle of 12 stars above the national identifier on blue background) no longer need a GB sticker when driving in European Union countries.

Glasses (spectacles): wearers must carry a spare pair in the car at all times.

Headlamp converters are compulsory.

Lights: dipped headlights should be used in poor daytime visibility.

Mobile phone use is illegal whilst driving.

Motorcycle drivers and passengers must wear crash helmets. Dipped headlights must be used at all times.

Third-party motor insurance is compulsory. A green card is not required but your insurer should be advised of your trip.

Replacement bulb set and fuses are compulsory, including any tools required.

Seat belts are compulsory for front and rear seat occupants, if fitted.

Visibility vests are compulsory if you have a breakdown.

Warning triangle is compulsory. One only is required for non-Spanish registered vehicles. Two for Spanish vehicles, but to avoid difficulties with the police two are recommend.

BRINGING YOUR PETS

Without a doubt this is an issue that comes up over and over for people living in Spain. A personal view of our experience on this is as follows:

First of all we brought our dog and cat with us when we travelled from our ex-home to our temporary home in Ciudad Quesada in 2006.

We travelled from Plymouth to Santander in our very old Hymer bought for the purpose. Travelling over night, our cat stayed in the Hymer with his food and bed. Our Westie was kennelled on the top deck where we had access to her at all times for little walkies and feeding. *We* were kennelled in a very nice cabin with full facilities.

This was in the early days of passporting but it was so easy I can't remember exactly where checks were done. I think it was the paperwork rather than the animals that were looked at.

The rules on passporting are different according to each country. Research is vital and don't just take your vet's advice but look at the information available for the countries you are travelling to or through.

Gatwick will, for instance, have planes to Alicante on which you can bring your pets passported accordingly. There are also some businesses who will sort out the whole process of shipping your pets for you. One thing is for certain, this is a pricey business.

Horses and ponies are even trickier – this has to be done through the military in Spain. Too complicated to be discussed here but not impossible by any means.

Within Spain people do travel by all forms with pets but do your research with the relevant authority.

In the same way you should always travel with water for your own needs remember the animal's needs too.

Beaches are also a thorny problem as most city beaches do not permit dogs on them. Dogs on leads when walking and some large dogs deemed dangerous may need muzzling.

Resources

Embassy T: 915 249 700

British Consulate Alicante T: 965 216 190

Dutch Consulate T: 965 212 175

German Consulate T: 965 216 022

CURRENCY EXCHANGE

www.currenciesdirect.com

www.escapecurrency.com - offer an FX Rate Tracker and foreign currency you can pick up at airports

www.hifx.com - one of the most well-known forex brokers

www.moneycorp.com

www.travelex.com

www.worldwidecurrencies.com - efficient personal service from this company based in London

DOCUMENTS

www.ehic.org.uk - information on the European Health Insurance Card and application form

www.direct.gov.uk/en/BritonsLivingAbroad/BeforeYou Go/DG_4000018 - report on benefits payable when you are abroad.

www.dnielectronico.es - electronic DNI

DIRECTORIES

www.yellowpagesspain.com - English directory offering a list of useful services.

www.paginas-amarillas.es - Spanish yellow pages with comprehensive listings. Also has street maps, restaurant and hotel directory

NEWSPAPERS AND MAGAZINES
In The UK

www.livingspain.co.uk

www.aplaceinthesunmag.co.uk

www.livingabroadmagazine.com

In Spain

In English

www.coastrider.net

www.costablancaleader.com

www.costablanca-news.com

www.euroweeklynews.com

www.inlandtraderonline.com

www.roundtownnews.co.uk

www.surinenglish.com

www.timspain.com

www.thisiscostablanca.com

www.yourlocalnewspaper.info

In Spanish

www.cincodias.com

www.diarioinformacion.com

www.diariosur.es

www.elmundo.es
www.elpais.com
www.hispanidad.com
www.laopinionpublica.com
www.publico.es

RECOMMENDED READING

James Burke, "The Day the Universe Changed" 1985, 0316117048

Cornwell Bernard, "Sharpe" novels on Spain and Portugal

Penelope Casas, "The Foods and Wines of Spain" Penguin Books 1985 revised several times, 0140466657

Giles Tremlett, "Ghosts of Spain" 2006 Faber and Faber, 0571221688

Jason Webster, "Duende" 2005 Black Swan, 0552999970

Debbie & Marcus Jenkins, "Going Native In Murcia", Lean Marketing Press, 1905430213

Simon Harris, "Going Native In Catalonia", Lean Marketing Press, 1905430302

Yolanda Solo, "Spain: The Expat Survival Guide", Lean Marketing Press, 1905430310

WEBSITES

www.alicantevivo.org
www.wikipedia.com
www.travelpod.com
www.dailyspain.com
www.expatica.com
www.gencat.cat
www.thisisspain.info

MORE LINKS

A complete and up-to-date list of web links to estate agents, language learning resources, hotels, travel companies and other useful contacts for visitors and investors in Alicante can be found at *www.nativespain.com*

About Susan Bearder

Susan Bearder is now semi retired but still exhibits as a photographer in Barcelona, London and New York with Galeria Zero. She will have a solo exhibition in Barcelona in April 2009.

She has been writing a blog for Native Spain.com for nearly two years and has caught the writing bug. She is also writing her partial autobiography under the working title "Letters to America" about her search as a War Babe for her American family. She writes for a European Gardening Blog/Forum called "Vistas from Afar".

Having MS she moved to Spain with her partner Steve in order to find a better quality of life. Good fresh food, a stress-free environment, a sense of harmony to surround her - all these things were prescribed for her by the medics and those who understand MS but were hard to find in the UK.

She initially lived in the Alicante region while looking for her dream home, the one that ticked all the boxes for her and her partner. The process was highly informative and put her in a position to write this first edition of Going Native in Alicante.

She now lives with Steve, his widowed mother (Fay) and a whole cacophony of dogs and cats on the Murcian-Almerian border.

If you'd like to interview Susan or get her opinion for a feature then email... *mailto:press@bookshaker.com*

Index

NativeSpain™.com

Be in our next guide...

We're committed to ensuring the quality of our guides and as such have set up a free membership site for readers and natives to share their hot tips and updates...

Find out all about Spain's towns, cities, culture, beaches, restaurants and more.

Use the diary feature to share your story, as it unfolds, with other expats and would-be expats in Spain. Learn from other people's successes and mistakes in the forums.

Join FREE, get involved and you could be featured in one of our printed guides...

Write your own guide...

We're in the process of creating Native's guides o all regions of Spain. If you're an expat now living in a new part of Spain and have a skill for writing then get in touch with us to find out more about author opportunities...

www.NativeSpain.com

A BRIT'S SCRAPBOOK

GOING NATIVE
IN MURCIA

SECOND EDITION

The Essential Guide for Visitors, Expats & Homebuyers

MARCUS JENKINS
DEBBIE JENKINS

FREE FLIGHTS TO BE WON

www.nativespain.com

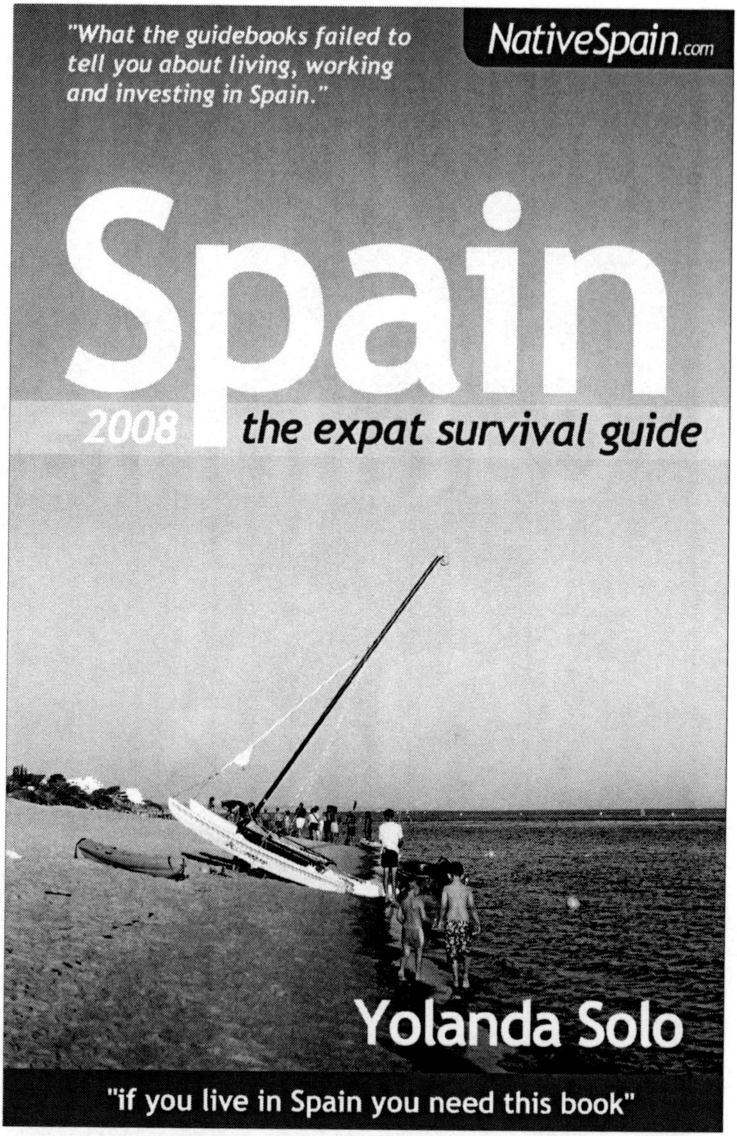

www.nativespain.com

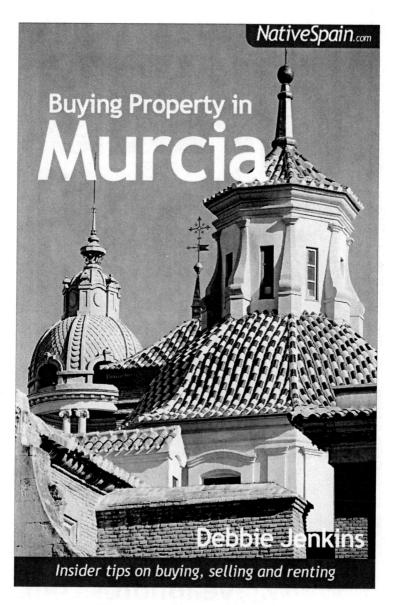

www.nativespain.com

People·Places·Culture·Vision
www.javeaphotos.com